PERFECT
MADNESS

PERFECT
MADNESS

*from awakening
to enlightenment*

donna lee gorrell

**INNER
OCEAN**

The names of the participants as well as some locations in this true story have been changed to protect the identities of the people involved.

Library of Congress Cataloging-in-Publication Data

Gorrell, Donna Lee.
    Perfect madness : from awakening to enlightment / Donna Lee Gorrell. --Makawao, Hawaii : Inner Ocean, 2001.

    p. ; cm.

  Includes bibliographical references.
  ISBN 1-930722-01-X
    1. Enlightenment (Buddhism)   2. Buddhism--Doctrines. I. Title.

BQ4398 .G67 2001
294.3/442--dc21   CIP

Inner Ocean Publishing, Inc.
P.O. Box 1239
Makawao, Maui, HI 96768-1239

Cover design: Beth Hansen-Winter
Cover art: Darren Hopes, Debut Art
Interior page design and typography: Beth Hansen-Winter
Editing: Barbara Doern Drew

Printed in Canada by Friesens

9 8 7 6 5 4 3 2 1

Contents

Acknowledgments   vii

Introduction: A Life before Life   1

CHAPTER 1: Breaking the Crazy Barrier   9
The hardest part about going crazy is getting there

CHAPTER 2: Rites of Passage   47
Surviving a pity party

CHAPTER 3: The Encounter   77
Leftovers, Milquetoast, and the greatest battle never fought

CHAPTER 4: Immersion   101
Sin and eternity in a bathtub

CHAPTER 5: The Worlds   129
The order of chaos and the wisdom of flowers

CHAPTER 6: The Goal   169
Much ado about everything

Epilogue: And the Beat Goes On   195

Notes   201

Bibliography   213

ACKNOWLEDGMENTS

I AM DEEPLY GRATEFUL TO MY HUSBAND, LARRY, FOR HIS MANY years of unending support and understanding, and to my sons, Glenn and Brian, for their faith in me. I would like to thank my draft editors: Andrew Zahn, Richard Tanski, Julia Hollister, and Nancy Newman (especially for her psycho-spiritual critique). I would also like to express my gratitude to Jeanine Kitchel, Dr. James W. Dilley, and Sr. Paule Freeburg for their abiding friendship throughout this project. I am forever obliged to John Elder, Chip McClelland, John Nelson, and Roger Jellinek at Inner Ocean Publishing for recognizing this work and providing encouragement to me through its transformation process; to Bill Greaves and Beth Hansen-Winter for the outstanding cover and interior design; and to Barbara Doern Drew, whose knowledge of the content and editorial skills have brought this book to a level beyond my greatest hopes. Lastly, this book could not have been written without words from others who have helped us understand why we are here. To those teachers, who have tasted the miracle of our existence and then shared it with the world, I am eternally indebted. Thank you all.

INTRODUCTION

A life before life . . .

I WAS NAIVE WHEN MY SPIRITUAL JOURNEY BEGAN. I WANTED growth without change, wisdom without experience, security without sacrifice, and life without death. I wanted to swim in the waters of eternity without getting wet. Instead, I found myself immersed in unfathomable darkness with no trace of where I'd been and no glimmer of where to go, lost in the void of my own mind and convinced I was going crazy. I had no way of knowing I was on a path to enlightenment.

The journey inward is magical as well as overwhelming, marvelous as well as miserable. When the human mind—which is our servant, not our master—tries to answer our cries for peace, let the games begin!

We find ourselves slipping deeper into uncharted layers of consciousness. Our comfort zone of sameness feels violated. One moment our mind is flooded with understanding; the next, on the brink of insanity. Self-doubt permeates our being, and we experience symptoms paralleling mental illness, even borderline psychosis. We wonder if the only difference between insanity and sanity lies in the ability to *be* crazy without *acting* crazy.

Terrified there is something wrong with us, we shun the very unity for which our soul hungers. We retreat from the spiritual experience because we don't know what a spiritual experience *is*. We see it as a problem instead of an opportunity.

To escape the problem of spiritual growth, we formulate alternate forms of craziness: fall into a destructive lifestyle, in love with a guru, in need with a psychologist, in greed for power, or in anger for a cause (something needs saving, and whether it's a tree, a soul, or a mosquito doesn't matter). However, all these efforts to avoid the original problem and keep defeat in abeyance are temporary—and this is good—because they're not satisfying.

Until we overcome the tricks of the human mind, we will not realize that everything we have ever wanted has been ours from the outset. But this is a difficult realization to achieve! We must first plunge into darkness and, with no footsteps to follow, work our way out. No one can tell another how to do this, for the path is to one's true Self.

Albeit in darkness, this path is not without guidance. It's simply a matter of being open to the clues—feeling, listening, and watching what is happening at every point in the journey. A subtle message, like a warm breeze through the caverns of consciousness, will usher us past danger. A memory—something we've read or heard—will give solace at the moment of our deepest despair. A vision may dispel confusion and lift us to a new level of understanding.

Whenever understanding is imparted, we can *trust* it. This calls for trusting ourselves and our inner senses, even when it seems we can't. Lastly, when the worst is at hand and we feel we've lost the battle for inner peace, we need to know that others have gone through the same process and arrived victorious at the Source of all creation.

We were not created to suffer, we were created to enjoy life eternal! But, in order to know this, we must *experience* it. Going to church won't make this happen for us, nor will reading, performing rituals, being a good person, leading an aesthetic life, or discussing ad infinitum the "Theory of Everything." It takes letting go of everything and making the journey inward.

At first, I was reluctant to write about the agonizing parts of the journey, but I realized that failing to do so would have nullified the purpose of the book, which is to dispel misconceptions about enlightenment while sharing my process toward it. We need to understand that enlightenment is *not* about getting happy. It is about understanding, renewal, transformation, acceptance, and, ultimately, surrender to the greatest part of our being, that which is eternal and creative, loving and omnipotent. When *this* is experienced, there are no adequate words to convey the ecstasy.

Along with details of my experiences, which are presented as they appeared to me at the time, I have included a retrospective—how I understand those same experiences today. In embracing ideas from the world's great religions and in sharing psychological perspectives along with the mystical, I hope to have woven a tapestry that will cover us all when we need it and that will disappear from our consciousness when we don't. As such, this book is meant to be nothing more than a guide to greater awareness of Self.

Perfect Madness began its life in the spring of 1991, almost two decades after my journey. I was trying to learn a word-processing program for my children on our new home computer. After I tired of typing "The little brown fox," I decided to practice with whatever thoughts came to mind. I was surprised at how suddenly I remembered what had happened between November of 1972 and July of 1973—a fantastic nine-month journey I wanted to write about at the time, but didn't know how to put its reality into words. I knew that words lied. Nothing could convey Absolute Truth. Even the memory isn't real. No truth is real but the Absolute itself.

When the typing began, I realized I didn't have to do anything but tell my story. I didn't need to make others believe what I believed—just be honest, I decided, and that would be enough. Before I knew it, I had a first draft. Since then, I've gone through three computers and countless word-processing programs.

While writing, I considered making consistent my references to God. But God did not always appear the same to me, so I decided many names would be helpful in expressing perspective as well as *feeling*. Conversely, I found a need for consistency when using pronouns. As such I have chosen the masculine when referencing God and the feminine when referencing a person. These terms, however, are not intended to ascribe gender. I use them in the generic sense.

I also considered that my journey may have begun long before the onset of my tale in *Perfect Madness*. As such, some history here of my spiritual background may provide additional insights.

When I was eight years old, I began reading books on psychology. I'd always wanted to know why I was here, why *any* of us were here. My parents couldn't tell me, neither could the nuns and priests at my school, no matter how they tried.

I suspected the answers might be found within my own mind. I also knew my mother had mental problems and wanted to find out more about them, so I borrowed *Fundamentals of Psychoanalysis* by Franz Alexander from my aunt's bookshelf. By the age of nine, I was reading Dante, Tolstoy, and Dostoevsky—Mother's suggestion, but I found them depressing.

When I was eleven, my parents divorced and I lived with my father and younger sister and brother. Within a year, we had a new mom, Arta—and a new life. Only then did I realize the normality we'd missed because of my mother's schizophrenia. We were finally a family like any other. Whew! And my father was happy, too. He had "peace of mind," as he put it.

I decided to start my search anew, this time at the beginning. I was convinced that my answer was written somewhere in a book, that humankind had overlooked it, and that I was going to find it. This meant the first of everything: Aristotle, the first logician (at least so I thought at the time), and Darwin, because he could tell me about the "origin of the species." I also borrowed a book from my uncle, *The Twelve Rules of Straight Thinking* by William J. Reilly, and from Arta, *The Logic of Language* by Bernard F. Huppé and Jack Kaminsky.

At fourteen, I was attending public high school and in the process of being confirmed Lutheran at the church where Arta taught Sunday school. I still did not know why I was here, though, and neither did Pastor Luke or Pastor Mark. Perhaps Freud would tell me. Maybe Kant, Sartre, or Nietzsche knew, or Plato, or Descartes (whose famous "I think therefore I am" I saw as pitiful: A duck quacks, therefore . . .). Some ideas I filed away as pertinent, others I discarded.

Einstein excited me, however. His relationship with the universe was intimate, open, and direct. He didn't frame what he saw with standards of acceptability, dogma, faith, *or* logic. Undaunted by the magnitude of his search, unintimidated by society, unimpressed with himself, and unashamed to *not* know, he opened his mind to the innocence of creation and bravely shared his findings with the world.

Around the age of sixteen, after a secret crush on my high school physics teacher (mostly because he understood Einstein) and a brief bout with atheism (during which I would not read a book that had the word *God* in it), I began studying Eastern religions. Hinduism worked into the practice of yoga, then came Buddhism, more psychology (mostly Carl Jung), psychodynamics (L. Ron Hubbard and Ernest Holmes), and some occult studies. I tried to connect the dots from one perspective to another as if all were equally viable alternatives to inner growth and understanding. But my Christian-trained subconscious echoed guilt about studying other paths. I needed a break.

My uncle lent me some motivational books, which led to mind power and positive thinking, which led to parapsychology, mysticism, and then Christian mysticism, which led me back to the Bible because Saint Paul was a mystic—at least I saw him as such. I'd gone full circle.

But then I had to compare Corinthians to the Gospels, then the Gospels to the Bhagavad Gita, and that to the Koran. By the time I was eighteen, everything had begun to mush together and I wasn't sure what I wanted to read anymore.

I'd recently graduated high school, had a boyfriend and a job at Aunt Mac's medical clinic in Chicago, and was deciding whether to attend medical school and become a doctor or to attend laboratory school and become a technologist. Either way, I

had to get on with my life. My questions, after all, were still un-
answered.

Then I met Bob Shapiro, my aunt's friend. We only had a
few moments together, but those few moments changed the direction of my life. He spoke of Zen Buddhism and told me his
friend Alan Watts had written a number of books on the subject.
The Way of Zen and *The Spirit of Zen* were the first two he sug-
gested I read; the list went on from there.

I felt like someone had given me a new toy! Zen was great
because I *couldn't* understand it. It was confounding and I was
determined to *get* it. Yet I did not know what I was going after,
except that it was called "enlightenment."

Within the next four years, I'd graduated lab school, married the boyfriend, taken a laboratory position at Chicago State
Mental Hospital, and devoured every Alan Watts book I could
find, then D. T. Suzuki, Robert Linssen, et cetera. If *Zen* was in
the title, I read it. As Zen is historically a combination of Taoism
and Mahayana Buddhism, I also read the Taoist classics, then
went deeper into Buddhism.

During these four years (age eighteen to twenty-two), I became involved with the theosophical writings of J. Krishnamurti
and H. P. Blavatsky, as well as Judaic mysticism. In addition, I
made sallies into the scientific world. New discoveries were being made in cosmology and physics, most of which I enjoyed
learning about. New gurus were all over the place, most of whom
I enjoyed *ignoring*. But I had to read their books, just to see what
they had to say, which was—in my mind—usually nothing.

I deplored a gurucentric mind-set. No guru was going to
dangle a carrot in front of my nose as if she had something I

didn't—at least not person to person. Books, yes—ashram, no! My only hope was that when I found truth, I would *know* it as truth.

I reached a point where my every thought, action, and feeling was examined, and if it wasn't "enlightened," it didn't count. My intellect was working overtime, scrutinizing and then devouring all that came into my path. Something had to give, and it did.

On a cold November day in 1972, my journey into the unknown began. Little did I know this adventure would take me to the ends of the universe and to the Source of all creation. In time, all my questions would be answered. I would gain an understanding of why and how we are here and eternal. I would learn that it is in eternity that we live, for we are cocreators of this universe—individually, collectively, and through the mind of God.

Chapter 1

BREAKING THE CRAZY BARRIER

The hardest part about going crazy is getting there . . .

THE CHICAGO BOUTIQUE BUSINESS WAS BURSTING AT THE seams. It was November of 1972; I was twenty-three years old, married, and business partner with my husband in a small women's clothing shop on the north west side of the city. While radio advertising, promotions, and buying trips to New York and Los Angeles left little time for recreation, Pete and I were relieved and happy that, in less than two years, "Mystique" had become a smashing success.

The storefront looked like any other one-story, display-windowed shop in the area, but its interior looked more like the comfortable parlor of an old Georgian house. Nineteenth-century wooden confessionals, purchased from a Catholic church, served as dressing rooms. Heavy scarlet-tasseled draperies were hung about, and the walls were adorned with old prints, paintings, collages, and posters. Racks of clothing, bins of jeans, and glass cases brimming with jewelry and purses surrounded the focal point of the boutique: a gold wing-backed couch, where customers would relax for a chat, whether they were shopping or not.

Pete and I lived nearby in a dormer apartment, which was quiet and cozy, filled with books and antiques, a place where I enjoyed reading and contemplating. This was my release from the demands of business. Pete's release was to have nights out with "the guys." The honeymoon was over, and I was striving for a comfort level in my two-year marriage. I was also striving for spiritual enlightenment. I trusted whichever came first would nourish the other.

On this cold November afternoon I had been reading D. T. Suzuki's *Essays in Zen Buddhism* at the dining room table. As I wondered why Monk Jōshu would put a sandal on his head to signify his understanding of Zen, I looked up for a moment and saw, in my mind, a wall. It appeared to be composed of stones of various shapes. The instant I questioned the meaning of this vision, my perspective changed and I could see the entire structure. Suddenly, the wall crumbled like a large building imploding from carefully placed explosives. It fell upon itself and disappeared.

With no noticeable jolt to the foundations of my psyche, I became transfixed on the darkness that lay beyond. I wondered what had happened and how such a barrier could have existed in my mind—a barrier I scarcely knew was there. I also had the immediate perception of having more mental space. This left me wondering, *Where do I go from here?*

> *To realize Zen one has to pass through the barrier of the patriarchs. Enlightenment always comes after the road of thinking is blocked.*
>
> **Zen master Mumon**[1]

As the days passed, I began to notice some difficulty in my thinking processes, and I had spells during which I felt thrust headlong into blackness. My being was helpless because there was nothing to support me—as if I had been taken to the far reaches of outer space and tossed out of a ship. The ship was my mind, and the space was outside. I had the shocking realization that I was literally *out of my mind!*

As this happened, the shadow entity that I had identified as my *self* spontaneously left its mental sphere and shot off into a place without boundaries—a place where there was nothing to grasp. I couldn't sort out why this was happening because my mental processes were shrinking to the point of uselessness. This new space was interspersed with my being, and I with it. I was losing control and was terrified. When a period as short as forty-five minutes passed without one of these spells, I was grateful. The fear of losing myself and being unable to return to my familiar mental state was almost overpowering.

Most disturbing was I had no confidence in my mind's ability to function properly. Something had been lost, and I did not know what it was. I began to look at other people and wonder how they could be confident of their perceptions of life. Since I could not trust my own sensory perceptions—is the doorbell *really* ringing, or am I imagining it?—I had no way of differentiating reality from illusion; there was no basis for confirmation. So if others were around, I usually let them be the first to mention things such as the television picture going fuzzy or the radio losing sound.

Losing the ability to confirm even seemingly unimportant events, however, carried with it a positive aspect: my mind was being cleansed. Like clouds dispersed by the wind, old beliefs and stale contentions began to vanish from my consciousness. Suppositions I'd taken for truth no longer orchestrated my actions. Gone was the nagging subliminal tune to which I had danced for my entire life. Responding to my own mind was becoming a choice, and this brought a refreshing sense of freedom.

As I became accustomed to the new inner space, I learned to function within it. But the more light was shed on the deeper layers of my consciousness, the more I began to doubt myself. This doubt became so overwhelming that my mental foundations—like the stone wall I had recently envisioned—collapsed. I had no feeling of direction or support and soon realized the only thing I could confirm was that I could confirm nothing.

Suddenly a Great Doubt manifested itself before me. It was as though I were frozen solid in the midst of an ice sheet extending tens of thousands of miles. . . . To all intents and purposes I was out of my mind. . . .

—**Zen master Hakuin**[2]

This confusion intensified from moment to moment, day to day, and week to week, until I reached a horrifying conclusion: I was going crazy! The thought that I could live without knowing what I was doing was more frightening than anything I had ever known. Going insane would be worse than never having existed.

The fear that there was something terribly amiss with the connection between my body and brain made me see my body as alien, not a part of me. I felt separate, disconnected, and alone, like a human trapped in animal form. I even saw my hands as grotesque paws. The shock of this horrified me and made me further doubt my sanity.

I didn't want anyone to know of my problems—not my

husband, family, or friends. I was afraid that if the image others had of me faded, I would have no expectations to meet, and I knew I needed those expectations. Human interaction was the gauge that measured my performance. In other words, if I was having a panic attack and didn't feel like going to work, I did it anyway. And some mornings this wasn't so easy. Out of the blue, intense terror could literally stop me in my tracks and I'd want to rush home. But just placing one foot in front of the other, refusing to turn around, knowing the dread could follow me anywhere—even home—allowed me to forge ahead.

I had to *maintain*. As a result, I made a vow of silence in regard to everything—every feeling, kernel of self-doubt, and fear I had. I would not speak of these things until my nightmare was over. I also vowed to continue with my daily life as if everything were normal, even if *I* wasn't.

Unusual physical symptoms also began to occur several times a day with unpredictability, growing more frequent as time passed. I experienced sensations around my skull that felt like painless electric shocks. (I termed them "pings.") They came in a series: if there was one, others followed within a few seconds. On many occasions, I had a distinct feeling of movement in my scalp and hair, as if someone were standing above me lightly brushing it with a hand. At other times, my brain felt sealed in a bowl of swirling water. In addition to this vertigo, I also experienced head-to-toe chills, itches that had no apparent cause, changes in my breathing and heartbeat, and alternating tingling and numbness in my hands and feet.

Had I been more concerned about my body than my mind, I probably would have been a regular at the doctor's office and perhaps labeled a hypochondriac. My preoccupation with my state of mind, however, overrode my physical state. As I continued to be thrust past the outer limits of my mind, I realized a journey had begun: the dark journey into myself. I did not know where to go, except further inward.

Normal activities became more difficult, as every fear I had ever known grew to monstrous proportions. It became nearly impossible for me to breathe when in an enclosed space, and several times I had to run from an elevator so as not to pass out. Even underground garages evoked visions of concrete ceilings crashing down. Since I'd never before experienced such irrational fears, I began to believe that it wouldn't be long—perhaps even the next moment—before my sanity completely ran out.

One winter night in particular was a nightmare of claustrophobia. Pete and I had been invited to a friend's apartment in downtown Chicago for an evening of tacos and old horror films. Our route through tunnel roadways made me increasingly uneasy, and when we parked in an underground garage the ceiling seemed to press me to the floor. After a suffocating elevator ride, we finally entered our friend's spacious apartment overlooking the city, and I could breathe at last.

Suddenly I realized to my dismay that the beautiful views were locked behind sealed windows. There was one small balcony, but it perched thirty floors above the street. Therefore, my choices this night were grim. Inside was suffocating, outside was frightening, and avoiding either was impossible. There was only one thing left to do: just let my *self* go wherever it was going. I let go. Surprisingly, nothing strange happened. It seemed that in constraining my consciousness I had exacerbated the problem. But contemplating the differences between complete abandon, conformity, and constriction would have to take place tomorrow. The lights went out, the movie began, and I spent the rest of the evening trying not to think much about anything, especially the trip home.

Within days, my claustrophobia turned into paranoia. At times it seemed the entire world was inside my head and I had no control over what went on there, but I thought everyone else did. Everyone else knew everything, and because they would not tell me what was happening, I suspected a conscious conspiracy to keep me out, separate and alone. There were also times when I believed my family and closest friends were simply indulging me until I went completely insane, then they would put me away somewhere. To say the least, I was confused, bewildered, and fearful that at any moment I would completely disconnect from reality.

This is where doubt saved me. It is a two-edged sword by its very nature. Once doubt enters to this degree, verifying *anything* is impossible. As a result, I doubted *everything*, even my paranoid suspicions. Nothing was concrete.

Still, I hoped that if I could act normal I might remain normal. As such, I feared that discussing my eroding sanity with family or friends would accelerate my mental degeneration. (Normal people didn't do that.) And I didn't want professional help—I had less trust in the psychiatric community than I did in my (albeit internally) hysterical self. This was probably because of my mother's illness.

My mother, Jacqueline, had her first breakdown when I was

The best norm for distinguishing the mystic from the neurotic is daily life.
—William Johnston[3]

three years old. Over the years, she underwent a number of shock treatment therapies in mental hospitals and was finally diagnosed as schizophrenic with manic-depressive tendencies. Memories of seeing her forcibly taken from the house in a straitjacket and of visiting her in hospitals filled with drugged people caused me to fear psychiatry more than madness itself.

Because I was afraid of sharing in my mother's fate, I resolved to handle my problem on my own. My vow of silence and my promise to carry on in a normal manner, no matter what, became my grounding. These two things also helped me to assess how well I was functioning on an everyday basis. If I had a paranoid moment, I remained silent about it. If I had a frantic moment and believed I was unable to perform a task, I forced myself to perform. The more difficult it was to keep my vows, the thinner I knew my thread to sanity had been worn. In addition, my underlying belief that no one is ever hopelessly insane sustained me in my most trying times.

I had worked with mental patients from the age of nineteen. The psychiatric wards at Cook County Hospital, where I received my laboratory training, were my favorite. I felt comfortable with patients (perhaps because of my mother's illness), almost as if I had known them in another time. But it was my working experience at Chicago State Mental Hospital that caused me to wonder what drove people beyond the limits of sanity. The patients who were not required to be locked in wards were permitted to wander the grounds, walk the halls of most buildings, and eat in the commissary with staff. Since we did not wear uniforms and usually took off our lab coats at lunchtime, it was at first difficult to distinguish the patients from the hospital employees—although the distinction was sometimes crucial. Personal safety was an ever-present concern. I quickly learned to tell the difference by simply observing the way everyone walked. The patients' body language spoke volumes. After a while, simply by observing their postures, movements, and facial expressions, I could discern the patients' prescribed medication.

The more I observed, the more I wondered how someone could be perfectly lucid one moment and delusional the next. There was an invisible line that, once crossed, temporarily unplugged them from reality. What they saw and thought was very real to them, and many were ready to battle the world to prove it. Other patients were often rational, bright, sensitive, and compassionate. They seemed like souls without guidance, lost in the realm of their own power and brilliance. I wondered if they had let their inner strength become their weakness.

Then there was my mother. She had learned to function in the contained society of mental hospitals but not in the real world. One afternoon my grandmother phoned me at work to tell me they were admitting Mother (who was then about thirty-nine years old) to Chicago State Hospital—no other place would take her. That day I had been working in the admissions lab, where all new patients underwent blood and urine tests. My grandmother said she was on her way there with my mother and that she would understand if I decided not to be present when they arrived.

I pondered what to do. I had trained my lab partner, Pam, so I knew she could handle my mother if need be. Furthermore, Pam was wonderful with all the patients. Then I remembered the times my mother acted like an angel because she actually thought she was one. I also remembered the times when she screamed at those around her in an effort to make them believe her delusions. I recalled the times her mind displayed its brilliance—her vast command of the English language, her erudition—and the loving moments we shared when she was lucid. I wondered what she would be like on this day, so I decided to stay.

I hadn't seen Mother in four years, and yet there was no warm reunion. Submissively she sat down in a chair, looked at Pam and me, then calmly told me I looked well. Her arms were thin and her face was drawn, but her thick black Cherokee hair, soft skin, and dark, almond-shaped eyes remained untouched by time. Repressing emotion, telling myself I would deal with it later, I introduced her to Pam, drew her blood, and told her I would visit her in her ward. As she sadly walked away with a white-coated attendant, I remembered the last time I had seen her in a hospital.

I was fifteen. She was at Elgin State Hospital, a horrid place about an hour west of Chicago. She was housed in a rundown cottage with windows that wouldn't open and doors that wouldn't close. She wanted to introduce me to her friends, so we walked over to a nearby building in the compound. The room, lit by only a single lightbulb suspended from the ceiling, had a long wooden table at one end. On top of the table were containers filled with plastic beads of all shapes, sizes, and colors. Seated around the table was a group of men and women working intently. One agonized over which beads to choose, another fiercely guarded her beads, and yet another struggled to string a bead, as if this were the most urgent task in the world.

When my mother held up the little string of beads she had made for me, I felt immersed in sorrow. I wanted there to be a difference between my mother and the others in this room, but there was none. I was beginning to realize that no one could help her but herself—not her genius-level IQ, her keepers, nor I.

So now she was hospitalized again—this time at the place where I worked. I knew it would not be a long stay, a few weeks at most. As she had done at Elgin, Mother would fool the doctors into believing she was fine. (She was smarter than most of them and *very* convincing when she wanted her way.)

As time went on, Mother gave me little peace during my workday. Rather than concentrating on beaded necklaces, she focused continually on the hairpins she was sure the other patients were stealing. I brought her a new package every day, but they were not suitable. She wanted *her* hairpins, the ones that had been stolen. Exasperated, I began refusing her calls to the lab (don't know how she managed that). I also refused to speak to the hospital director about the threats she claimed she'd received from other patients. I said, "Mother, get over it. I've been spat on, peed on, bitten, punched, groped, chased, and had my car rewired by a patient who decided I shouldn't go home. Even so, I face these patients every morning with a needle in my hand. If I can manage, so can you."

That gave her something to think about, but not for long. Soon, she had me at my wit's end. Emotionally, I had learned to protect myself from Mother when I was eleven, and now, at age twenty-one, I was having to do it again. I felt like I was backsliding into my past.

My parents divorced when I was eleven, and my father was awarded custody of my sister, Margie, then seven; my brother, Ricky, three; and me. My maternal grandmother, Maw Maw, had always picked up where Mother had left off. Our new apartment on Lyndale Street was only seven blocks from Maw Maw's place, so she helped care for us until my father married Arta, which was the following year. With this marriage, I felt as if a heavy weight had been lifted from our family, for Arta brought serenity and happiness to us all. I no longer had to play the role of mother for my sister and brother—we finally had a real one.

My father, Richard, always taught me that everyone has some sort of disability, some imperfection. He would not accept my criticism of another person, even when he may have felt the same way. "Are *you* perfect?" he would ask. He did, however, warn me about people who were "emotional vampires." In his Tennessee drawl he would say, "Sometimes, honey, you just have to remove yourself from the situation." As to concepts of right and wrong, his guiding hand pointed me inward for the answers: "Use your best judgment," he would counsel. When my judgment proved inadequate and I had to get myself out of a jam, I heard, "Can't never could do anything," which to me meant "can *can* do anything." I came to believe that within the physical laws of the universe, I could accomplish *anything* if I set my mind to it.

Daddy was my first spiritual mentor. From him, I learned self-discipline, a prerequisite to inner growth. The power of the mind over the body and the importance of peace of mind were subjects we often discussed. The concepts that nothing is more powerful than the mind and nothing is more painful than not having control over it were beliefs ingrained in me from an early age. Later, when everything else seemed wiped away, his teachings would hold me steadfast. The man who protected me from my mother's madness also saved me from my mother's fate.

My Aunt Maxine—or Mac, as we all called her—was the other great influence in my life. Mac was my mother's twin sister, but two people could not have been more different. She handled my mother's erratic behavior with her own strong intuition and personality. She'd had a lot of practice—from the cradle onward. With a persona reminiscent of Rosalind Russell in *Auntie Mame*, Mac exuded a charming self-confidence that I could not help absorbing. When I was with her, I felt nothing could upset my "applecart." If something was troubling me, she would say, "When you're dead it won't matter. Why should it matter so much now?"

Accepting reality and moving forward in life was Mac's gift. She had a different approach from my father's, but their goal was always the same: Get some enjoyment out of life, even if you're sitting in a pile of cow dung. Recognize your choices, and either take a liking to the smell or walk away.

Well, Mother walked away from Chicago State Mental Hospital within a few weeks, as I suspected would happen. I walked away a year later because I needed to be at my shop full time. Though I missed the patients terribly, I had no idea that within barely a year, my questions about the line between sanity and insanity would become personal. I was twenty-three years old, had a relatively new marriage, and a new career. But no longer would I be able to stand apart from the mental patients I had known, or even from my mother, for I was becoming one of them. I was approaching the *other side*.

In trying to develop a new way of thinking and understanding, I had been thrown past my usual intellect into the unfamiliar.

The barrier had been passed, but my ability to operate in a new realm was yet to be developed. Paradoxically, after passing the barrier, I looked back upon it as only an illusion.

In Zen this wall is called the "gateless gate" or "gateless barrier." According to contemporary Zen master Zenkei Shibayama, "When he has actually broken through the barrier, he can for the first time declare as an actual fact that it is gateless. He is then wholly free. . . ."[4] The problem was, I did not know what to do with the freedom.

Another problem with passing the barrier was that initially there *was* no new understanding. There was only a darkness that eluded all attempts at mental formulation. It could not fit into patterned thinking because it was patternless. Compared to my usual mental activity, it was motionless; and compared to ordinary life in the manifest world, it was boundless. And yet this was not really a place. It was a consciousness to which my awareness had awakened: the *void*.

I felt as if I had reached the top of a ladder and could not back down because I did not know which way down was. I did not even know where I was standing. My sense of knowing a position relative to *anything* was lost in the void because nothing could be taken into my consciousness to be objectified. In fact, the reverse was true: instead of taking ideas into my mind and digesting them, I was thrust into an abyss in which there was nothing to digest. If anything, I felt it was the abyss that would do the digesting. The only reality was dark space.

The concept of the void is not confined to the Zen discipline or any other school of Buddhism. References to it can be found in many different teachings, from ancient alchemy to contemporary mysticism, and descriptions of it are as varied as the perspectives from which they come. The anonymous author of the fourteenth-century masterpiece *The Cloud of Unknowing* wrote of the void: "Don't worry if your faculties fail to grasp it. Actually, that is the way it should be. . . . It cannot be explained, only experienced. Yet to those who have newly encountered it, it will feel very inscrutable indeed."[5]

The void is not only difficult to explain, it is indescribable. Nevertheless, I conceive it as *consciousness without cognition*. Whenever we take a thought into our mind (whether or not we are aware of it), we have a thoughtform—something we can grasp, think about, play with, ponder. In the void, however, this is impossible because the void is untouched by the separational processes of thinking. It cannot be torn apart or delineated because it is pure, patternless, unfettered consciousness—the mind unattached to ideas. Ideas are limiting, but the void cannot be limited. As contemporary Belgian Zen scholar Robert Linssen explains, "'Void' should be understood as the absence of values arising from attachment and identification."[6]

The void is simply what is left when all else is gone from the mind. This is not to say, however, that there is nothing there. In this universe, there is no such thing as nothing—for everything is of the essence of its Creator. Even nothing is something. As is written in the *Hermetica*, the writings attributed to the ancient Egyptian alchemist Hermes Trismegistus (ca. 100 B.C.), "Nothing that is, is void. . . . no such thing as void exists, or can have existed in the past, or ever will exist."[7]

The void just *seems* void. It appears as vast, dark emptiness because the mind is unaccustomed to the space beyond the gateless gate. The mind will soon learn, however, as ninth-century Chinese Zen master Huang Po understood, that the void is truly the "realm of the real *Dharma*" (ultimate Truth).[8]

Detachment is a harrowing process whereby we pull the leeches from our soul. When we no longer need to identify with mental objects, we become aware of our previous programmed thinking patterns, though we may not know how to repattern our thinking. Nevertheless, our focus changes. We are no longer satisfied with the extraneously temporary and strive for the intrinsically permanent. Above all, we recognize and reject the human habit of blind deification. This is when we search for God with open eyes, and the lesser gods—money, selfish love, pride, vain control—are pushed aside so we can get a clearer view in our search. However, there is a problem with this—namely, whereas blind deification results in dissatisfaction or disappointment, the refusal to blindly deify may push us to the brink of insanity.

✢   ✢   ✢

If anyone knew there was something wrong with me, I thought it would be Pete. I'd reached the point where I could no longer assess my behavior and needed a heart-to-heart with him. I was also afraid it was only a matter of time before I went completely mad, and I wanted to prepare him for the worst. I broke my vow of silence.

It was a Sunday evening in January. Pete and I had just returned home from work and I was wondering what to make for dinner. Suddenly the lights went out. The neighborhood had lost power and no one knew when it would come back on. I thought this might be a good time to talk. I was willing to put my soul on the line—expose myself and allow my every weakness to be explored. I trusted him—I had to.

When I mentioned I was having problems with my thinking processes, that perhaps I was—like my mother—schizophrenic, Pete laughed. He told me that whatever problems I had were imaginary, then left me in the dark to go out with the guys. A black moment in my life had gotten even blacker.

All right, I thought, first order of business: Don't burden an already strained marriage with minutia. If Pete didn't think I was crazy, I certainly wasn't going to fight about it. Second order of business: dinner!

I went to a nearby pizzeria to gorge myself, but couldn't eat. I sat at the service counter with a cup of coffee and thought, *Perhaps it's best Pete doesn't think there's anything wrong with me. That means I'm doing OK. I'll never mention it again. He wasn't cruel or scoffing, just self-absorbed. Perhaps I'm self-absorbed.* As I rationalized ad infinitum, I wondered if my marriage was fulfilling—or empty as my tummy. I had no way of knowing which was the case; the ability to assess simply was not within me.

I was caught in a schism maritally, but that was, I contended, a reflection of what was happening to me psychically. I decided that if I could fix myself inside, everything would be OK *outside* as well. So I was forced to consciously combine the inner world of psychic experiences with the physical world and its events. And I had to do this while keeping my vows: *maintain silence* (never again to be broken) and *continue to function* (as long as possible, no matter what the future might hold).

My small apartment became my private asylum during the winter of 1972. I felt separated from the rest of the world, from all things familiar, as the battle for peace and sanity began. Disconnected and alone in my inner universe, I fervently attempted to reconcile my mental world with the outer world, but somehow only separated them more. Unable to dance to an unfamiliar tune, my intellect was no longer serving its role as protector and governor of my mind. It had become subjugated to something greater: *awareness*.

Although my awareness expanded in direct proportion to the diminishing dominance of my intellect, there was a problem. Awareness did not know how to *do* anything. That was my intellect's purview, for it knew things; but my awareness had no information. With nothing to use as an operating base, I was compelled to participate in life with no clue as to what I was doing.

While I managed to appear to function normally, I did not know *how* it happened. I was aware (cognizant/mindful) of what I was doing and what I'd done, but those actions were not pursuant to a preprogrammed format we would commonly perceive as intellectual. This was discouraging, humbling, humiliating, and frightening.

It seemed I was a mere observer to my actions rather than an actual participant. Sometimes I felt a thousand miles away from Earth and my small body was a microscopic puppet controlled by a magical will. Other times, I felt immersed in the material world such that the input from my senses left little room for mental expanse. The difference, or distance, between these two extremes was a schism. The similarity between these two extremes was that *rationale* was precluded in both. And yet I was aware of what was happening, not only in the world around me, but in my mind—a vast wasteland of consciousness, dark and foreboding.

Precariously perched atop a mountain of fear, I realized that I had to find a way to consciously assimilate my inner and outer worlds. The only alternative was psychosis—a complete disconnect from reality—and I did not want to end up there. In fact, I was very close to psychosis because now all of my fears had grown to monstrous proportions and were hiding in dark corners of my mental labyrinth, waiting to spring. In running from my fears, I had learned they only grew larger. Therefore, these monsters had to be faced.

The first monster I had to stare down was my dependence on others for self-esteem. This was a big one, for it involved denying myself the need for approval—I *feared* not having it. As a result, some relationships with family and friends had to be adjusted, but for the better. My expectations diminished and I could give energy to others rather than sap it from them. My next monster was the need to be needed, another was intellectual pride. As I continued this process, I finally understood my monsters were merely old identifications, each with the same name: *ego*. The monsters we face and the battles we fight to rid the mind of them are probably as varied as our personalities. Each of us has our own kind of craziness.

At the same time, each soul has its own sense of reality. As no two individuals can stand in the exact same spot simultaneously to admire a tree, it follows that no two individuals will see that tree exactly the same way. There will always be a different perspective. Sometimes these differences are so small they go unnoticed; other times, they are large enough to cause wars.

When one outlook is so distorted that the tree is no longer even a tree, we tag this condition mental illness. We say this person is out of touch with reality, that her connection to the real world has been broken—in short, that she is delusional, psychotic. Well, perhaps she isn't.

Throughout history, some of the greatest thinkers and spiritual leaders have arrived at some point of madness, but instead of stumbling into complete craziness they pivoted inward to further understanding. They learned to observe, feel, and let life continue without judgment. They learned how to fuse what they saw in their mind's eye with the reality of the outer world. They learned how to become their own teachers and their own students. Keeping nothing for themselves and willing to endure the pain of the inner journey without retreat, sometimes they were exalted, sometimes they were crucified. Neither really mattered, for they knew they were living in the truth of what they were.

Life is a process of the unconscious becoming conscious. The mystic participates in this process by choosing neither side over the other as reality. This results in *integration with* life. The schizophrenic, however, widens the schism between the inner and outer worlds, which results in *segregation from* life. In a number of psychological studies comparing the mystic and the schizophrenic, there have been similarities in hearing voices, having visions, and encountering psychic forces. Psychologist Kenneth Wapnick's comparison of Saint Teresa of Avila's mystical experiences with schizophrenic episodes reveals the major difference between the two states of mind: the schizophrenic, unlike the mystic, is incapable of integrating her inner experiences with everyday life.[9]

The difference between mental illness and the mystical or

transcendental experience simply depends on our ability (or will-ingness) to deal with life as a whole. Seeing things others do not is not the principal issue. What is important is the way we trans-late and incorporate those experiences into ourselves. Just as one room of our house does not disappear when we walk into an-other, mystical experiences need not sever us from reality if we understand them as a means of exploring the same reality we have always known.

In *The Politics of Experience*, British psychiatrist and noted author R. D. Laing affirms there is really no such condition as schizophrenia.[10] Laing sees the psychotic episodes of the so-called schizophrenic as simply visions of one who has journeyed in-ward and gotten temporarily "lost." In relating the schizophrenic experience to the transcendental experience, he wrote,

> *Perhaps we will learn to accord to so-called schizo-phrenics who have come back to us, perhaps after years, no less respect than the often no less lost explorers of the Renaissance. . . . [One day we] will see that what we call "schizophrenia" was one of the forms in which, of-ten through quite ordinary people, the light began to break through the cracks in our all-too-closed minds.*[11]

Understanding psychosis is as difficult for someone who has been there as it is for one who has not. The only way to understand it is to be in both places at once: to let our minds operate on a level of intensity to the near exclusion of the outer world and to function in the outer world as if nothing odd were happening internally. Psychologists might call this "dissociative disorder," but there is not a complete break between the two worlds since there is a continuing effort to maintain a balance and achieve some sense of integration. The intensity with which we explore the inner world should be equally balanced with our desire to remain in the outer world.

If, for a moment, we try to comprehend that there is indeed no separation between things seen and unseen, between things in the physical world and those in the mental world, we will see that, in fact, *all* things are the spiritual world. This vision has been the goal of every great religion. Those who have learned that all things are the spiritual world have seen truth.

When we see nothing but truth, we simply see the world as it is. We see it through our own eyes, not through someone else's view or explanation. Without asking another to do the work for us—which means resisting the comforts of dogma—we experience the beauty of truth within and without. This is when the sense of schism dissolves. There is no opposition, no conflict. There is no more separation; there is union.

As for myself, the reality of this union revealed itself only sporadically in mystical experiences that opened and expanded awareness in both the inner and outer worlds. Sometimes I knew I was progressing toward deeper understanding and saw the accompanying pain as a by-product of gaining fuller awareness. Other times, I became angry with the universe for handing me a crash course in reality. Ultimately, however, my efforts changed from maintaining sanity to something more profound: gaining understanding.

> *Madness need not be all breakdown. It may also be breakthrough.*
>
> —R. D. Laing[12]

❖ ❖ ❖

I felt fortunate to be in close contact with my family at this time. My sister worked full time at the store and successfully managed things when Pete and I were away on buying trips. Many years of sibling rivalry had matured into a close friendship, and we could talk about most anything. But, as sisters usually do, Margie and I still compared ourselves to each other. Although our physiques were similar, her features were more delicate than mine. To me, she looked like a petite version of Grace Kelly, with her blue eyes, blond hair, and innocent smile. A little nervous and easily excitable, Margie graciously maintained I was smarter than she and of stronger character, although I never knew what she meant by that. I found her character quite strong and loving. Though she never knew it, she was a great comfort to me during this time of vicissitude. She made me laugh.

My stepmother, Arta, managed the bookkeeping, and my brother, Ricky, worked at the store part time. While I was surrounded by family and friends, I could not talk of my inner problems. I became torn between hope and despair.

Reading had always helped me better understand problematic situations, but now even the solace I had once found in psychology, philosophy, and even spiritual books was waning. The doubt in my soul would no longer allow that type of consolation. Despair was prevailing; depression was settling in. I slept fitfully, afraid of not waking up in my body. I thought perhaps I might awaken in someone else's body, or floating in the dark void of my mind.

Dawn always came as a relief, because its coming meant I had survived one more night. Yet the thought of what lay ahead filled me with dread. Moment-to-moment survival consumed my energy, and I grew tired from the struggle; there were times I felt I would surely lose the battle. I saw no reason for what was happening and desperately begged God for release. I hadn't asked much from him in the past because I hadn't thought I was in need. But as it became increasingly difficult for me to walk, swallow, or stop from shaking, I realized only he could help me.

I had no intention of medicating myself. Drugs seemed to constitute no more than an addictive Band-Aid that would only prolong the inevitable. Instead, I became a meditate-a-holic. Meditation was the only thing that would counteract the fear-produced adrenaline raging through my system; the temporary respite it provided permitted me to regroup mentally, physically, and emotionally.

However, the practice soon began to rule my life. Often it was necessary to rush to a bathroom or closet, and meditate away an irrational fear in secret. Feeling a desperate need to regain some inner balance, I would excuse myself from conversations with customers, buying sessions, dinners, and phone calls. Basically, I wanted to excuse myself from life, but I couldn't. I *had* to function. If I lost my normality, I would have nothing left.

Even the simplest tasks began to require my total concentration. I was a walking, talking bag of nerves. Moreover, my nighttime dreams were beginning to happen in real life. The dream world of my unconscious had become interspersed with my conscious world, and sometimes I couldn't tell the difference. Dreams, memory, and imagination were indistinguishable from actual events. For example, if I remembered a dinner party, I would not know for certain if I had attended it, dreamed it, or was seeing it before it happened. I was, at least, grateful for the awareness that

I was having this sort of problem—one more reason to remain silent about my situation: normal people weren't confused about such things.

At this point in my life, I was a mess. My mind could not control my body, my body could not control my mind; both were in turmoil. My body shook so badly at times I actually had to hide from people. Sometimes my heart palpitated, and I literally forgot how to breathe, swallow, or sleep. Finally I realized there was a driving energy within me that needed direction. I decided that since neither my mind nor my body could control the other, the only way to find peace was to control the energy.

However, I was not sure what this energy was. Although I had read about kundalini in yoga theory, it did not occur to me that there was a connection between it and what I was experiencing. I did not picture myself as going through a spiritual maturation process—I thought I was going crazy.

While there are a number of physicians and psychologists who now acknowledge the psycho-physical effects of the kundalini process, psychiatrist and ophthalmologist Dr. Lee Sannella is credited for pioneering much of the research in this area. In *The Kundalini Experience*, he correlates symptoms of mental illness with the kundalini process—a natural energy release that affects the body as well as the mind and spirit. He wrote, "Of those undergoing the kundalini process without preparation, not a few tend to feel quite insane, at least at times. By behaving normally . . . they may avoid being labeled schizophrenic, or being hospitalized, or sedated."[13]

Dr. Sannella's view is consistent with yoga philosophy: the

kundalini process is a symptom of spiritual maturation—a natural process—upon which the introduction of medical techniques cannot improve. Again, from *The Kundalini Experience*:

> *We must . . . help them recognize their condition is a blessing, not a curse. Certainly, we must no longer subject people in the midst of this rebirth process to drugs or shock therapy—approaches which are poles apart from creative self-development and spiritual maturation. . . . [They] are already undergoing therapy from within—a therapy that is far superior to any that modern medicine could administer from without.*[14]

Basically, he is saying that there is no "cure" for spiritual growth. But why should we want one? we might validly ask.

According to yoga theory, kundalini is a primary energy force that rests coiled at the base of the spine. There are seven main chakras, or energy centers, through which the kundalini progressively flows: the base of the spine, the lumbar region, the solar plexus, the heart, the throat, the middle of the forehead, and the top of the head. As the last three chakras (throat, forehead, and top of the head) are activated, or "opened," there is a more conscious realization of the workings of the unconscious mind and of the universal Mind, which encompasses all of creation.

Expanding consciousness is a progressive process. Yet once kundalini is activated, like liquid

When kundalini *is completely awakened, this power works by action and reaction to activate the* chakras *and thus gives progressive enlightenment.*
—**Rammurti S. Mishra**[15]

vitamins stored up from birth, it goes shooting through our spiritual nervous system and our consciousness is forced to work *with* it or it will be overtaken *by* it. Moreover, kundalini will not tell us what it is doing because it does not know. Only we know, and it is the job of our consciousness to figure it out. This is the progressive part of the process, sometimes known (especially in yoga theory and the "Northern" schools of Zen) as "progressive enlightenment." The "Southern" schools of Zen (Rinzai in particular) do not agree with the idea of progressive enlightenment. According to them, one is either enlightened or not—it's an all-or-nothing situation.

Based on my own experience, however, there is progressive channeling of the kundalini energy up through the chakras. Activating the first six chakras brings *illumination*, but one must activate the seventh (*sahasrara*) chakra in order to fully experience *enlightenment*. I believe one progresses *toward* enlightenment during this process, though enlightenment itself *occurs all at once*. Plainly stated, it's like being pregnant and then having the baby.

While we may not at first understand what's happening as kundalini channels through our chakras, we feel its *power*, which can precipitate all sorts of physical and mental symptoms. Some are a normal part of the process of awakening, and some are the result of trying to stop the flow of energy through the chakras. Kundalini can throw us into a state of anguish if we do not attempt to accommodate it. The feeling of losing one's mind, the nervous state in which the body finds itself, electrical pings in the skull, itching, vertigo, and sleeplessness can all be a result of kundalini activation. These symptoms are not imaginary. They are *real*.

When one assimilates kundalini, awareness expands. This can include seeing parts of our physical body as unfamiliar, even alien, as if we'd never seen them before and they are not really a part of our body. As internationally recognized physician and yogi Rammurti S. Mishra describes it, "One day you will see your arms are really relaxed and you will begin to feel consciousness separate from your arm, and your arm is in *yoganidra* [a state of complete bodily relaxation while the mind is awake]."[16]

Once kundalini is unleashed, enormous changes take place within. Proper channeling of kundalini is always translated into spiritual understanding. However, before we become comfortable with this process, we may have unsettling encounters with the unknown. The integration of the inner and outer worlds is the unconscious becoming conscious. Since the entire universe is our unconscious mind (as we will soon see), the fun is just beginning.

✣ ✣ ✣

I had no idea my kundalini had been unleashed, much less how far from my usual mental realm it could take me. Perhaps I would have been less fearful had I known this, but I'm not sure I would have been able to make the correlation between my experiences and the kundalini process. In any case, I would *still* have had to go through it. Once kundalini begins its work, like the Energizer bunny, it keeps going, and going, and going, and . . .

I still was not sure what was happening with my mind, yet I was still managing to function. Tuesday was my day off from work, and I usually shopped for groceries around noontime. One Tuesday in March, with about half of the shopping finished, I was standing at the supermarket meat counter looking at a T-bone steak when, suddenly, I *became* the steak! And that's *all* that I was—a butchered animal lodged in a cold meat counter, ready to be bought, cooked, and eaten. I did not see myself from the outside as such, but from the inside, I felt my being intersperse with each molecule of the steak, each space between the molecules. Then, bound into that form, I felt suffocated in a dark pool of mud. I was lost inside this strange dimension of matter until something, a *feeling* of sorts, reminded me of myself. I desperately wanted to be *me* again, but there was a huge force opposing my return.

I don't know how long I stood at the meat counter in a state resembling catatonia, trying to overcome this force and restore my consciousness. Fighting for my life—calling upon strength I didn't know I had—I felt as if I were swimming up Niagra Falls. Then I realized I'd made it. Filled with anxiety, but finally back in my body and able to think, I rushed to the checkout counter to get home as soon as possible. However, standing at the cash register with checkbook in hand, I felt a thousand miles away and began to see the store, the people, myself, and everything else around me as unreal. No longer could I apprehend reality. I had lost it. In a silent panic, my soul screamed to whatever spiritual guide was with me, to the universe, and to God himself: "I don't know what is real. Please help me!"

Stupefied, I could not move, think, feel, or hear. Everything stopped at that moment. All was still as I felt my feet merge with the floor. Then out of the silence, I began to hear something—not words, but a feeling-sound whose meaning I had to translate. My attention was completely focused on this message, which I knew could help me return to reality, yet it was outside of my grasp. "What is it I need to know?" I pleaded silently. "Tell me!" Then I focused on my body, my breath. As the rustling sounds of paper bags fell upon my ears, the answer came: "Now is all that is real."

I looked around the crowded store, then at the clerk who was waiting patiently, and I felt as if *truth* had been laid beneath my feet. And it was something that nothing—no force, no person—could ever wipe away. It was, and is, Now! From that point forward, this would be my reality. It had to be. It was all I had. Now.

On the way home, I looked forward to meditating, saying some prayers, then contemplating how to prevent myself from getting lost in objects. I knew that since it had happened once, it could happen again. I also wanted to hold onto Now as my reality. If I meditated on this to the exclusion of everything else, it would be so simple to live the rest of my life in only the reality of Now, no matter what confusion the inner and outer worlds brought. The answer to combining these worlds had been explained: Everything lives in the moment of the magnificent Now. I was shown in the grocery store that figuring out what was real and what was not didn't matter anymore. *Now is the only reality* became my internal mantra.

What I learned from this experience is that physical matter is not just outside of our minds, it is also inside. When we look at the world, we are seeing our own mind. The sole distinction between the two is the *concept* that we are separate from what we envision. When we are consciously pulling together the inner and outer worlds, we should not be surprised that there are times when we will spontaneously realize ourselves not only *in* matter, but *as* matter.

After this incident I was re-lieved to get home, as it had be-come my refuge. The apartment was a quiet, warm, and safe place. I usually meditated in the living room on the antique camel-back sofa Pete's grandmother had given

> *In each one of us,*
> *through matter, the*
> *whole history of the*
> *world is in part*
> *reflected.*
> **Teilhard de Chardin**[17]

us. However, the peaceful solace I had known in meditation had recently been broken with increasing frequency: flashes of unfamiliar faces appeared inside my eyelids, and sounds such as bells, chimes, and thumps distracted me. But I was learning to ignore the noises, acknowledge the faces, and then dismiss them as irrelevant. I intuited they were just hanging around my psyche because they had nothing else to do and that to interact with them could be detrimental. As mystic author Evelyn Underhill stated,

> *The great mystics . . . are unanimous in warning their*
> *disciples against the danger of attributing too much*
> *importance to "visions" and "voices," or accepting them*
> *at their face value as messages from God. Nevertheless,*
> *these visions and voices are such frequent accompani-*
> *ments to the mystic life that they cannot be ignored.*
> *The messengers of the invisible world knock persistently*
> *at the doors of the senses. . . .*[18]

I went deeper into new realms with each meditation. Al-though these meditations were not always enjoyable, I had no choice—I had to meditate as surely as I had to breathe. I knew that if I could not survive in meditation, I could not survive in life. I knew that meditation is life in a different form of expression, a purer form. When not meditating, I felt as if my mind was wearing dark glasses, the kind that prevent clear vision because there are distorted images mirrored on the inside. But in meditation the glasses were removed, and I could observe life from a perspective unobstructed by the confusing reflections of my busy consciousness.

During frightening meditations, I would fall into a trance and have visions. They seemed real for I was actually living them, just as one lives in one's dreams—until waking up. The difference between visions and dreams, however, is that visions feel far more real.

During one vision, I saw myself as an active participant in some sort of sacrificial ceremony in which a group of robed people were standing in formal arrangement around a large table in the middle of a cave. Lighted with torches and candles, the walls reverberated with a recitation from the robed ones, whose faces I could not see. As curiosity directed my focus toward the table, I could see a draped figure. Suddenly I became frightened something evil was about to occur, perhaps a ritual sacrifice. I then awoke from the vision. I was back in my own living room, had slipped into a trance, and was reciting the unfamiliar chant I'd heard in the cave. (I have not since remembered the chant, nor have I wanted to.)

As days passed, I realized the safety of my own home had been violated, for I perceived menacing forces around me—cold, dark, heavy, and negative. My thoughts turned to violent acts against those I loved, and I saw blood on my own hands. I also saw myself being ripped apart, as if I were drawn and quartered or on a rack in a torture chamber. I knew the negative thoughts were not conjured by my own mind just as I knew the visions weren't real, but I did not know where they came from and I didn't know how to battle them.

Then it occurred to me these menacing forces were entering my mind via *thought*. Thus, if I didn't *think* their way in for them, they could not get to me. I decided to guard my mind, every waking moment. Still, if I focused in one direction in an effort to protect myself, there was another force behind me. My unseen enemies were lined up along the boundaries of my consciousness, waiting for an instant of opportunity. If I ran, I knew they would enter.

One evening, surrounded by the forces, I was getting ready for a dinner out with Pete, my sister, and her boyfriend, Mick. My guard was up, and I'd managed to keep the negative energies in abeyance while bathing. With a sigh of relief, I got out of the tub and leaned over to give it a last wipe. Suddenly one particularly strong force seemed to come out of nowhere and almost knocked me to the floor. In a panic, I prayed for help. Suddenly, the words of Jesus (Matt. 5:39) rang in my mind: "Resist not evil."

I finally realized that to fight evil is to increase its power. The moment one engages in battle, she has already lost. Not to fight is to remain unmoved. I had been fighting these entities and had been losing. Thus, I resolved that remaining without resistance was to be my course from this point on. There simply was no other choice.

I knew there would be future encounters with negative forces, but I felt better equipped to handle them. I now had two precepts to use as survival tools: *Now is the only reality* and *Fight not evil.*

Fighting any adverse condition only increases its power over us, because we are making a reality *of it.*
—**Ernest Holmes**[19]

My sporadic insights into the phenomenal world were sometimes difficult to integrate into everyday life because they seemed without context, like a painting without a canvas or water without a glass. I soon realized my experiences could not be properly integrated until I had surpassed the level of awareness where they had taken place. Only then could I look back at them with enough detachment to apply the valuable and discard the impertinent—a task that would have been less daunting at the time had I been aware that certain spiritual disciplines identify similar phenomena.

Yoga theory, for example, calls the sounds—bells, chimes, thumps—that some people hear during meditation *nādi* and describes them as the physical manifestation of the pure energy of the universe, or *prana.* (All things are a form of prana, even kundalini, which is prana on a vibrational level more specific to the individual, like a fingerprint or voice pattern.) Yoga counsels us that focusing on nadi cleanses impurities from the mind. As yogi B. K. S. Iyengar wrote, "This is where the yogi is asked to concentrate upon the inner mystical sounds."[20] As to the faces or astral bodies seen in meditation, we are advised by physician, author, and yogi Rammurti S. Mishra to "not pay any special attention to them."[21]

In Zen, the term sometimes used for these phenomena is *makyo*—basically, illusion with a little validity thrown in for good measure. They are a "mixture of the real and the unreal," according to contemporary Zen master Yasutani:

> *Many makyo involve the hearing. One may hear the sound of a piano or loud noises, such as an explosion (which is heard by no one else), and actually jump. . . . He may see the Buddhas and Bodhisattvas. Penetrating insights may suddenly come to him. . . . yet from the Zen point of view all are abnormal states devoid of true religious significance and therefore only makyo.*[22]

And yet it seems the more mystical or psychic experiences we survive without letting our mind snap, the stronger the experiences get. This can be an unending battle unless we overcome the experiences, and the way to do this is simply by not placing so much emphasis on them.

When we are caught in this double bind, it is not easy to find a way out. Mirrors do not choose what they reflect, thus they reject nothing. If our mind is to learn anything at this stage, it needs to remain undiscriminating and innocent in its function by rejecting nothing and—like a mirror—holding to nothing. In keeping no images, no matter how ugly or beautiful, we remain unmoved and unbroken.

> *Avoid cluttering up the mind with such nonsense by letting it function as a mirror that only reflected what passed in front of it and nothing more.*
> —**Zen master Bankei**[23]

✤ ✤ ✤

Life on a tightrope is the best way to describe the weeks that followed. I was not sure what was happening to my mind, or why, but I was still *functioning*. If I were indeed going crazy, I wondered, why hadn't it happened by now? Perhaps my condition might not result in insanity after all. Fear became tempered, and I implored God for guidance and protection. He had already answered my prayers and given me tools for survival. While I understood he could not place me back in the cradle of my old mind, for I myself had left it behind, I hoped he would guide me through the trials that lay ahead.

Walking on a tightrope—strung between a world of matter and a world of visions—eventually caused a discernible change in my perception of the schism. Sporadically it began to disappear. During these peaceful interludes, my mental and physical worlds blended and I felt momentarily at rest. I could see life as a paradoxical mixture of interchangeable levels of reality, where the only difference between the inner and outer worlds was in the *illusion* that there was a difference. Most important, I could see there was something pulling it all together for me, something that imparted strength and peace. Yet I did not know what this something was. Although I continued to have inner battles, my tools for survival—*Now is the only reality* and *Fight not evil*—and the peaceful moments of security enabled me to keep in touch with everyday life.

Then, one afternoon in late March, something extraordinarily pleasing occurred. I was sitting in meditation, cross-legged on my living room couch with pink foam-rubber curlers in my hair, when I saw someone above me, quietly watching. Upon looking more closely, I saw it was *me*. Suddenly I realized I had been asleep my entire life. It was a very quiet moment—no questioning, no sound, no exclamation, no ecstasy, no reaction. There was nothing but a calm and pervading reassurance that strength and peace were all around me.

I knew what had happened. I had *awakened*.

I became water and
*   saw myself a mirage*
Became an ocean, saw
*   myself a speck of*
*   foam*
Gained Awareness,
*   saw that all is but*
*   forgetfulness*
Woke up, and found
*   myself asleep.*

Sufi poet Binavi Badakhshāni[24]

Chapter 2

RITES OF PASSAGE

Surviving a pity party . . .

A LTHOUGH I HAD AWAKENED TO A STRONGER AND CALMER SELF, I was quite depressed. My mental foundations had been removed. I tried to soothe myself with the notion that depression is normal when there is loss.

I needed to adjust to a new pace of life because I could not walk, talk, or think as before. Each thought, each breath, all movements of my body demanded total and properly directed focus. Concentration was impossible without complete physical relaxation, and relaxation required yogic breathing.

I had practiced a form of self-taught yoga since the age of sixteen, when I discovered a worn little book in Aunt Mac's large library. Upon opening its tattered cover, I saw it was *Fourteen Lessons in Yogi Philosophy and Oriental Occultism* by Yogi Rama-charaka.[1] Beneath it was the penciled inscription "Property of Richard Lee." Although my father had never talked to me about yoga, this was his book. Out of curiosity as much as respect for my father's ease in handling my mother's illness, I began my study of yoga.

My father didn't have much to say to me about the process except, "Be careful. Yoga is nothing to play with." Later, I discovered that, during meditation many years earlier, he'd had an

out-of-body experience in which he had been afraid of not returning. At any rate, he had attained a level of yogic adeptness.
Arta confided that he could relieve her migraine headaches simply by placing his hands on her head in a certain way.

I was grateful for having had this introduction to yoga because now was a time when its benefits were crucial: I finally
experienced the important connection between the body, mind,
and breath. When concentrating on my breathing, I could function without shaking. Attentive breathing also helped resist the
ever-present urge to run down the street screaming, "Damn it,
get me out of this mess!"

Almost a season had passed since my problems had begun,
and I hoped the coming of spring would bring a new season of
growth to my soul. I had learned much since that cold November
day when the wall collapsed in my mind, yet I still had more to
learn—or *un*learn, as seemed more the case. Although prayer
helped, meditation was the best way for me to objectively observe my thought processes. But since I couldn't sit down and
meditate all day, I learned to meditate *in action*. I used this type
of meditation throughout my daily life—working, talking, driving, or cooking. I no longer needed to sit in order to meditate.
Nor did I need to run to a bathroom or a closet to meditate away
a fear, as I had done in the past.

Yoga teaches control of the breath (*pranayama*) and accentuates observation of natural breath without letting the intellect
interrupt. When the mind and body are unified by the breath
connection we find quietude. Resistance to ideas disappear and
we are no longer required to ponder, mentally organize, or con

tend with perceptions. Yet life is not suspended in this state; rather, awareness of life is expanded.

Meditation is the state *preceding* rational thought. Words breed cerebration, which breeds separational thinking, which breeds more words. "The ultimate Reason itself is without words," according to Zen patriarch Bodhidharma (d. 532), "but to give expression to it, words are borrowed."[2]

Meditation in action is simply functioning and moving about in life without being drawn into thinking. (The art of t'ai chi is a good example of meditation in action.) We are aware if thoughts arise and we are aware of moving about, but that awareness—more potent than thought—also knows there is a part of ourselves, the spirit, that is not moving at all.

When one comes to a threshold of expansion in meditation, there comes a time when the intellectual mind is not capable of following. . . . the intellect puts a limitation on where this expansion is trying to go.

—Emmanuel's Book[3]

During meditation in action the body effortlessly shifts to accommodate the slightest motion. Initially, one must focus on maintaining balance. But when the body learns to operate in conjunction with the stillness of the mind, balance takes care of itself. In fact, there is really no difference between the body and mind in this state, for a constant exchange of soft, flowing energy unifies the two.

This energy, *prana*—Chinese, *chi*; Japanese, *ki*—comes from the breath. As I mentioned earlier, prana is the undifferentiated energy of the universe that is experienced individually as kundalini.

When kundalini is properly channeled, it filters through our consciousness as wisdom and understanding, or *prajña*. Thus, energy *becomes* understanding! When one has learned to meditate in action, sitting meditation is no longer necessary.

Meditation in the MIDST of action is a billion times superior to meditation in stillness.

—**Zen master Hakuin**[4]

Prayer also unifies us with the something *other* within our being. In a sense, prayer is a projection of our image of God; with this projection a form of communication takes place. Ultimately, however, there is no something *other* within our being. The more we pierce the illusion of separation, the closer we become in consciousness to that which we really are: the Self of all.

The less we objectify, the more real God becomes. We actually become closer to that Reality from which, through which, and in which we were created. There is no more potent tranquilizer than to focus one's breath and no better source of patience than praying. Prayer is the voice of our inner self reaching for the true Self, and vice versa. In the deepest sense, we do not pray *to* God, we pray *with* God. "God listens not to your words," as Lebanese poet and mystic Kahlil Gibran wrote, "save when He Himself utters them through your lips."[5] Hermes Trismegistus adds, "It is thy Word that through me sings thy praise; for by thee, O Mind, is my speech shepherded."[6]

Moreover, lest we confuse ritual or devotion with prayer, there is no particular way we *should* pray. We need not douse ourselves in holy water, get on our knees, cover or uncover our heads, prostrate ourselves, figure out what a bad person we've been all week, or separate our group by gender before getting down to the serious stuff. Prayer is a way of tuning the soul so it may harmonize with more expanded levels of consciousness in order that it may receive understanding, guidance, and, ultimately, fulfillment—not only for ourselves, but for those around us.

It seemed the more I prayed and meditated, the more unfamiliar my world became. My uneasiness, however, was soon balanced with a sense of being guided. (Spiritual guides are considered by some to be imaginary, but it does not matter. What matters is the guidance.) I could not see my guides in the material world, but I sensed their presence and my mind received their messages. I felt like a blind child walking in an unfamiliar place, guided by a loving hand. There was no choice but to trust. There were also times they chided me—not to degrade or embarrass, but to yank me back into correct ways of thinking, as a parent with a child.

The first time I noticed the chiding was during an evening of conversation with Pete, his sister, and her boyfriend. I was going through a phase where it was difficult for me to be around people who talked incessantly. It seemed the words spewing from the boyfriend's mouth were putting my brain into a spin; besides, I didn't like what he was saying. He was pompous and self-righteous, and I just wanted him to be quiet. But before I could interrupt him, someone or something stopped me. I couldn't utter a word. While the boyfriend babbled on, I realized a message was coming to me that I needed to comprehend. Suddenly, I understood: "This man's hunger to express himself is greater than your need to reproach him. Keep silent!"

I didn't second-guess this message, didn't wonder from where it came. I knew. One of my guides was helping not only *me*, but those around me. How loving, how wonderful! The next moment I looked at the boyfriend from a new perspective: I felt compassionate toward him. And I was a happier person for having listened to my guidance.

On another occasion, it was an hour before closing time at the store. For no seeming reason, I grabbed the keys and headed for the front door. Just as I was ready to turn the key, I realized it was not yet time to lock up. *How silly of me!* I thought, and went back to my paperwork. Within minutes, five young men came rushing in, filled their arms with clothes and rushed back out the door. Ricky, who was working that afternoon, went after them, and I later found him semiconscious in the back alley. He was fine, but we both would have been better off had I listened to my guides, who had tried to tell me to lock up.

Also, I learned I was often simultaneously in touch with one, two, or more guides depending upon my situation. I could discern different personalities through a blend of characteristics such as serious, happy, informative, frivolous, or stern, and remember if I'd encountered that particular essence before. The more familiar the combination, the more easily I could identify the guide. But this was unimportant activity in the scheme of things. Again, what mattered was the *guidance*.

Still, the occasions of knowing I was not in this alone were often tempered by some new psychic or mental experience that could rekindle fear and desperation. Frequently, I felt thrown into a time warp, as if the memory connection between myself and the world had been erased.

Often this happened on my way to work. Even if I could remember where I was going, I might not know how to get there. Driving around like a lost mariner searching for the familiar, I often wondered if anyone else was in the same fretful condition, destined for nowhere. In the end, my senses always found a way to make the mental connection; however, I would have to quiet my mind and concentrate on my destination in order to maintain my bearings. Remaining mentally still became very important.

I concluded I was experiencing a physiological deterioration of my memory connections. My mind was degenerating to the extent I could no longer remember how to remember; the operating pattern was no longer present. Although this was disconcerting, I eventually learned that my pattern had become the limiting template that prevented me from seeing the original, natural, and eternal beauty of Reality.

Experiencing reality involves change in the deepest sense of the word. Although I wanted to remain in the comfort zone of sameness, the harder I grasped at it, the more distant it became. I could see no reason for my memory loss, but it was necessary that I learn to relax with it. I had no choice.

One beautiful April morning

You [humankind] insist upon focusing your attention upon the similarities that are woven through your own behavior; and upon these you build a theory that the self follows a pattern that you, instead, have transposed upon it. And the transposed pattern prevents you from seeing the self as it really is.

—Seth Speaks[7]

as I was driving to work, it happened again. My store was a trip of about two miles from my apartment, in the neighborhood where I had grown up and gone to high school. Without warning, everything around me—the buildings, the streets—assumed a strange glow. I was in the warp again and disoriented. As I drove aimlessly trying to find my store, something completely unexpected occurred.

A thought, an answer as to my destination perhaps, came to my mind and hung there without meaning—as if it were another language needing translation. Although I was exasperated and tired, I could not let this pass; I needed to understand this thought. Suddenly, the decoding was innately there, and I was able to comprehend the strange dialect of this internal language! When translated into words, the answer was that I was not going crazy; rather, I was "out" of my mind—where I was *supposed* to be. The message continued: "Going outside one's usual mind is the beginning of spiritual growth."

I was seeing things anew for the first time. I understood that if indeed the spiritual world is new each moment, that was why things appeared strange. Another message came through: "The physical universe is not separate from the spiritual." This made perfect sense to me and explained my memory lapses. My mind—inseparate from the spiritual world—was also new each moment. But I did not like having no continuity with the past and was afraid of what was yet to happen.

"Great, God," I snapped, "if this is spiritual growth I want no part of it. Forget it and return me to normal." I was angry. I had been frightened for months, then forced to see that spiritual growth, or understanding, was the opposite of what I'd imagined. Spiritual growth, I'd thought, was supposed to bring peace, joy, and contentment. Instead, I was unable to stay in my body, getting lost on my way to work, getting lost in objects, surrounded by weird forces, and deprived of sleep.

Although I was angry, these messages puffed my ego. It had been my life's dream to understand why I had been created—why any of us had been created—and enlightenment would give me the answer; if not enlightenment, then perhaps God would give me the answer. I thought that if I could endure these trials just a little longer, I might reach my goal.

Curiosity and ego inflation then mobilized, causing me to believe that if my quest continued, it could be done at my own pace—I could choose when and where my experiences would occur. But this presumption was soon obliterated, along with every other frivolous conviction I held precious. The walls of my mind had crumbled and attempts at preservation were as useless as trying to turn ashes back into wood.

The experiences of being lifted by new insight and hope, while wondrously beautiful, were almost always followed by an intense fear of never knowing what would happen next. One moment I felt I was in heaven and the next in hell, and if this was to continue, I had to find another way to handle it. After much self-examination, I observed that the visions of being out of my mind, lost in the dark space of the void, only appeared when I *thought* of myself. This was quite a revelation! All I had to do was quit thinking of myself and my problems would be over. At long last, the refusal began.

I had never thought I was addicted to anything, but when I tried to stop thinking of myself, the realization of my absolute

Our usual "I" is a false and impotent image. But just as this phantom cannot actually will or do anything, it cannot get rid of itself.

—Alan Watts[8]

addiction to thought swelled within me. I saw that I was subliminally glued to every thought that passed through my mind—habitually riveting my self-image to every mental perception and then deciding if I wanted it to be a part of me. I was doing this without even *knowing* it.

Then the reality that this self-made image might not really be me began to surface: perhaps I was no more than a transparent monarch upon an intellectual throne, arrogantly delivering one foolish, empty judgment after another.

Increasingly I saw how we project our *idea* of self into thought, then—to reinforce that self-image—we *respond* to thought. We live as if we are what we *think* we are, without ever knowing the thinker. As Robert Linssen wrote, "Our accumulations of memories seem to attach themselves to us to such an extent that constant vigilance is necessary if we are to free ourselves from their clutches. . . .[9] The function of the mind is not to store up memories but to understand the process of its own functioning in the Present."[10] And internationally known philosopher and lecturer J. Krishnamurti concurs: "Be aware of the ways of your own mind, and you will discover . . . the mind forms habits in order to be secure, safe, certain. . . . Memory is a habit. . . . The mind moves from the known to the known, from one certainty to another; so there's never freedom from the known."[11]

With close observation I could see how hilariously limited thought is. Deluded by this phantom world we've created, we wonder why life is unfulfilling. Yet we refuse to let go of thought because we fear we will go right along with it (like throwing the baby out with the bath water). We believe the image we have of ourself is *real*.

"Thought cannot possibly ignite the flame which changes man,"[12] according to Krishnamurti. If this is the case, what then can ignite that flame? Where is the transformative ability for humankind? It lies in the only place it possibly could: beyond our accumulation of memories, beyond *thought*—outside our perception of what's rational, outside our *mind*.

Awareness exists before thought enters the mind; thus we can be aware without thinking. But when we *do* think, we forget that thought is our individual translation of experience—a representation. We then confuse the representation with the original experience.

While creatively or destructively thought can help to shape reality, it is always something *other* than the reality it represents. Thought originates from that which already *is*—it is a by-product of reality, not the reality itself. As the revered wisdom teacher Sri Nisargadatta Maharaj said, "Abandon false ideas, that is all. There is no need of true ideas. There aren't any."[14] Meanwhile, those things called "ideas" take form.

> *The interval between the mind's passing from one idea to another—the period of calm between the two storms of Thought—may be described as the native condition of Self.*
> —Yogavasishtha[13]

❖   ❖   ❖

It was quite a jolt when thoughtforms were first shown to

me. These little pockets of energy dangle about in the collective unconscious and can be seen by the mind's eye before entering individual consciousness.

It was a beautiful night in Chicago. Pete and I were on our way to dinner at John and Mary's house. John had been Pete's best friend since high school, and Mary and I had become close. As we drove, Pete and I managed strained conversation about the weather. I was keeping to myself the tales I had recently heard from customers about his infidelities. His time at the store was decreasing and his nights out were increasing, but I didn't have the wherewithal to confront him. Besides, he would have admitted to nothing. So I tried to think positively and convince myself the stories weren't true. Through the car window I saw a fat yellow moon rising brilliantly over Lake Michigan—and with it went my soul.

Suddenly I realized I was out of my body again, floating with "clouds" all around me. One of these clouds entered my mind the way vapor enters a vacuum bottle. But unlike vapor, which would assume the shape inside the bottle, my mind conformed to the amoebic shape of the cloud, which I realized was the thought that I had that moment processed. The next moment, I was back in my body, left with the understanding that thoughts exist separately from our souls. They are, however, intrinsically connected to our mental realm, and our brain is the receiver.

I also learned that thoughts gravitate to a more inclusive source. Like air bubbles that pop and disappear when they reach the surface, thoughts disappear when they reach the level of truth. And just as we have the ability to take a breath of fresh air and expel it underwater, we can inject a thought with higher understanding and then rethink it for humankind. Doing so transforms a skewed or incomplete thought into one that ascends to truth.

Forgiving another for a transgression is a good example of this process. In the very act of forgiving, we acknowledge that the source of hurt does not demand our resentment. Forgiveness frees us to grow beyond what has been done to us. It is the key to release for both the transgressor and the transgressed.

A completely open mind can accept absolutely any thought without abhorrence and see *through* it to the end, where there is truth, untouched by thought processes. But this is not so easily recognized if one is entangled in thought, for thought cannot see beyond itself. With this new understanding, I could see no purpose in thinking. It had nothing to do with truth. Thought itself was becoming my enemy.

I began "brain cleaning" on a regular basis. Whenever I caught myself hopping from one thought to another, I'd stop, take out my pretend broom, and sweep until there was nothing left for me to

> *Having established the mind in the Self, let him not think at all.*
> —Bhagavad Gita[15]

think about. Then I could resume my place on a firmament of clear consciousness. The more I did this, however, the less I was able to find a firmament. Soon I felt as if I were sinking into my own consciousness. No thought could save me, for thought was not *real*.

Sometimes there seemed a hurricane in my brain and I was caught up in its torrent; at other times, I was in the still eye of the storm, waiting for the next surge. One day the passage "Judge not, that ye be not judged" (Matt. 7:1) resonated within me. The words were turned around, though, to say, "Judge ye not thyself." I soon learned that identifying with *anything* is judging one's self.

As sixth-century Zen patriarch Sêng-ts'an wrote in his celebrated poem "Inscribed on the Believing Mind,"

> *The object is an object for the subject,*
> *The subject is a subject for an object;*
> *Know that the relativity of the two*
> *Rests ultimately on the oneness of the void.*
> *In the oneness of the void the two are one.*[16]

I realized that if I stopped objectifying myself I would no longer need to judge myself; "the *relativity* of the two" go hand in hand. My journey, difficult as it was and would continue to be, did not call for my assessing a position relative to *anything*. I understood what Saint John meant when he stated, "If I bear witness to myself, my testimony is not true. . . ." (John 5:31).

I distilled my problem: the difference between self and self-image. One was real, one was illusion, but I didn't know which was which. The deeper I delved into the concepts surrounding self and self-image, the more naked and overpowered I felt—and there was no place I could hide, for the negative forces that had invaded my awareness without permission had come back with a vengeance. Moreover, this underbelly of human consciousness was becoming more vile and terrifying than before.

The forces around me were almost overpowering. Although I could not actually see them, their presence was vivid. When I personified and demonized these parasitic forces, they had the ability to surreptitiously enter my consciousness and trigger a malignant form of mental activity. When I refused to accept their horrid thoughts as mine, my thinking patterns became so twisted and convoluted that the level of confusion was almost intolerable. My brain felt like a radio where all of the stations were playing at once.

Other times I saw what these forces could do to others. Like a living nightmare, I had visions of agonized souls—tortured, screaming with no sound, crying with no tears—pleading from the depths of the abysmal crevasse into which they had been cast. Through their eyes I could see all of the pain, selfishness, ignorance, and hopelessness in the world. I wanted to ease the sorrow and give release, but was completely powerless. I was coming to understand that although one can carry another's crippled body, each soul must walk on its own, mine included.

It did not matter whether I was working, watching television, reading, or talking when I had these experiences. While I was able to meditate them away, I was unable to identify what triggered these baleful sights. Then it occurred to me that if I learned about them while remaining detached, they would stop. Somehow I needed to observe—without judgment—in order to learn.

Progressively, I had learned that Now is the only reality and that fighting evil gives it more power; then that the physical world is not separate from the spiritual; and next that *thought* is somehow enmeshed with the projection of *self* into the void. I began to see that the less I judged things (including my own visions), the less power thought had over me and the more I began to see things differently. What we would normally consider mundane suddenly took on a spiritual quality. I was beginning to have mystical visions with increasing frequency.

At first the visions were subtle, taking place in the morning hours when my mind was uncluttered and refreshed. Something as simple as the tree outside my dining room window revealed a brightness I'd never before appreciated. Reaching innocently toward the sky in its nakedness, vulnerable yet strong, it was perfect in every way—and it was telling me so by showing me its unabashed magnificence. Such visions began to expand into the inanimate as well, encouraging an intimacy with the world around me. I was boundlessly grateful to God for the revelations.

Alternation between the onset and the absence of this joyous transcendental consciousness . . . [is] the characteristic intermediate stage between the bitter struggles of pure Purgation and the peace and radiance of the Illuminative Life.

—Evelyn Underhill[17]

At times my visions may have given outside observers the impression that I was in a catatonic state at one moment, then brimming with silent passion the next. While I saw mystical life as a crash course in reality, I realized my compulsion to share this reality with others carried the dangerous presumption that I was the only one who saw truth.

Moreover, mystical insights seem almost insignificant when translated into words. Words do not carry the experience; they are simply fingers pointing to it. In *The Mystical Way*, Christian mystic and author William Johnston characterizes this predicament: "[The mystical experience] is an expanded or altered state of consciousness and to explain it in terms of the ordinary day-to-day consciousness that makes up our language is almost impossible. Language from one state just does not fit the other."[18]

Around the time my mystical visions began, Rachel, one of my regular customers, came into the store. With glazed eyes staring vacantly, she told me about the importance of cardboard egg cartons. "No one realizes their benefit to the world or how significant they are in the entire scheme of life itself," she proclaimed. At first I thought she was joking, but then she fervently rambled on, "This world would be a better place if only everyone would collect them."

When she asked me how many cardboard egg cartons I had, I knew something was terribly wrong. If indeed Rachel had had a mystical vision concerning cardboard egg cartons, she was having a problem assimilating it. Because she was exclusively focused on the *object* of her vision instead of the *message* of her vision, she had become overpowered by it. (Whatever that message may have been, I doubt that it was: Rachel, deify cardboard egg cartons.) I felt sorry for Rachel and understood her predicament, but did not know how to help her. A week later I learned she had been committed to a mental institution.

Fortunately, unlike Rachel, I was almost always dumbstruck after a vision—at least long enough for me to realize how ridiculous I would sound if I yielded to the temptation to blurt out what I had just seen. Although my visions were sometimes so strong that shock seemed the next step, silence prevailed. I soon learned, however, that mystical visions carry a secondary message that tunes the mind and soul for harmonizing the experience with everyday life. But sometimes it takes patience and focus to incorporate such messages. Getting carried away with any vision before it is assimilated is "not seeing the forest for the trees." The trick is to accept truth and get on with the challenging business of living with it.

This I had yet to learn—and from an unlikely situation. Perhaps I subconsciously chose being in public to gain insights, but there was an unusual significance for me attached to grocery stores, particularly the meat and produce sections. They provided the atmosphere for a number of mystical experiences that gave me a peek at an expanding reality in my life: God.

When the newness of this reality first overwhelmed me, I was in the supermarket shopping for produce. Without warning, I fell into a catatonia-like state—again. Immobilized, I was lost in communication with the amazing generosity of God's bounty. The array of foodstuffs—lettuce, pears, corn, tomatoes, peaches, and apples—was mounded upon table after table in mesmerizing, geometrical pyramids of color. I could see the overpowering love and benevolence of our Creator before my eyes. Manifested in the food was the very body of God, and it was *alive* with his love.

For the first time I was completely lost in the love of God. There was no urgency to return from this vision, as when I had gotten lost in the T-bone steak, for I had learned that matter is a form of God, veiled only by our ignorance. When ignorance is dispelled, he is seen everywhere in true communion with us. I remembered the words of Jesus, "For my flesh is food indeed and my blood is drink indeed" (John 6:55), and sud-

It is the Lord who has brought the cosmos out of himself.

—Shvetashvatara
Upanishad[19]

denly understood that with every bite of food we take, we *are* feasting on the very body of God.

The return from this vision was a gentle float back to recognition of my body and its surroundings. Still a bit spellbound, I looked at shoppers around the market and wanted to shout, This magnificent bounty has been created for us! God is alive. He loves us. Can't you *see* it?

But I held my tongue, and instead tears welled up and emotion overtook me. It was a deep, passionate feeling I couldn't identify, for it felt like all my emotions were exploding at once. I looked inward for help. Finally, the secondary message came to me through the thought-feeling language that I had come to know as "gnosis" (our innate ability to know and experience truth): *Gratefulness is not required—gifts are given out of love.* In that moment I knew that all we need to do is recognize the source of things. Seeing and accepting is enough—the rest will flow through us naturally. Bluntly translated: OK, so you've seen a glimpse of God's magnificence. Now get on with your life!

Afterward I wondered about accepting and giving. The Bible says, "It is more blessed to give than to receive" (Acts 20:35), but I was experiencing that it was *easier* to give than to receive. Receiving was difficult! At least it was for me. For in order to receive, I first needed to be willing to accept truth without knowing exactly what that truth may have been. This meant I could have no barrier between it and me, no resistance, and no hidden alternative available in case I didn't like what I saw. In other words, if I wanted understanding, I had absolutely nothing to say about what I'd get for the asking. I was learning about humility—and when God's love is felt, it is profoundly humbling.

Through these daily experiences, I began to see emotion as something real and more powerful than the things of the material world. I also saw that although there appear to be many emotions, there is really only one. Our delusion that there's more than one is due to our limited vision and inability to translate the cosmic language of gnosis. There is a word in every language for this emotion. In English it is, of course, *love.*

These words and gifts make me so extraordinarily embarrassed when I recall what I am . . . that more courage is necessary to receive these favors than to undergo the severest trials.

—Saint Teresa of Avila[20]

By now, my intellect was almost shut down. Maintaining stability demanded that I resist the mental urge to feed myself with conclusions; I needed to suspend judgment. All I could do was feel, then release the spiritual truths that passed through my soul. I learned, in short, that the intellect inhibits our gnosis. Why? Because gnosis stems from intuition.

When we search our memory for a particular word and the word pops into our mind, we recognize it. We *know* this is the word we were looking for. With gnosis, we search our soul for an answer and what comes forth is an impression, a feeling. If we are receptive, this feeling will translate itself into understanding. But this kind of understanding has nothing to do with the intellectual process. It is received in a flash, intuitively, and it is *potent.* We know—without doubt—what is true or untrue.

This gnostic process became the sole medium through which I could communicate with God. The similarities between it and what I'd read about "speaking in tongues" led me to understand them to be one and the same. There is a communication before words, needing no translator, needing only the soul's ability to discern what is conveyed. When we listen, there is no doubt of the message from the soul's teacher.

There were, however, many things I could not understand. Within my soul there still raged a fierce battle. I had no idea who was fighting or even why, but—like rumblings from deep beneath the earth that portend natural disaster—I could *feel* it. I sought safety on my mental tightrope, but my surroundings were becoming blacker and I wasn't sure of my steps. Beneath me was the underbelly of human consciousness, the negative forces I had kept in abeyance. There was no escape, no real peace, except for the sporadic insights that gave me the inspiration to go on.

Spring was in the air, but the tree outside my dining room window was still bare. I wondered if a horrendous storm had destroyed the newly formed blossoms and I hadn't noticed. My work continued, as did my marriage, though I was preoccupied with thoughts of death. While I knew this would *eventually* be my fate, I could not understand why I was so afraid of dying *now*. Yet, in looking deeper, I realized my fear of death was no different from my fear of the unknown. Whatever it was that fueled the desire for divine knowledge—enlightenment—also told me the experience would erase my fear of death, because the unknown would then become known. Everything would become a part of my conscious awareness and I thought that meant that then I could choose what was to remain. But there is a problem with this way of thinking: the farther one goes past the intellect, the deeper one goes into the unknown, where there is no choosing. There is only acceptance—a willingness to understand, without judgment, the truths that are revealed.

Once spiritual truths are revealed, they cannot be turned into a system and still remain true. Religious institutions want to teach and we want to learn, but in the process we may forget that Absolute Truth is not in books—it is *within* us. As such, spiritual truth cannot be dogmatized or objectified; it can only be experienced. Yet we are afraid to experience truth—alive, energizing, and beautiful as it may be—because the act of doing so calls for our relinquishing control and accepting whatever it tells us. Truth dispels illusion and leaves only what *is*. But we are afraid to see what *is* because we don't know if we are going to like it or not, so we distance ourselves from reality and live as if we are a character in a movie, all in an effort to retain the precious illusion that we have control over existence.

> *When do you choose?*
> *Only out of confusion,*
> *when you are not quite*
> *"certain." When*
> *there's clarity, there's*
> *no choice.*
>
> —J. Krishnamurti[21]

I, too, wanted control, but was finding the more I attempted to seize control, the less of it I had. I was beginning to understand that we cannot feel alive until we accept the pain of the character in this self-created movie. Until we shed the limiting ego protection and break through the barriers of the mind, we cannot see truth.

Somehow I knew the *I* in me was false—only a compilation of memories, a delusion—but I *felt* truth all around me. There was, however, no clear vision of it because of the battle raging within. However, glimpses of insight caused a revolution in things seen as well as unseen. What I had thought to be real was slowly becoming an *old* reality. Life as I had known it was fading like a song where the melody lingers, but only in the mind.

I had to rely more and more on my gnosis, which had become more acute, to let me know what was real, absolute. Even my recent preoccupation with death went completely out the window one Tuesday in late April. I'd just finished putting away the groceries and was on my way to make the bed when I noticed something strange about the bedroom door—it was no longer just a door. It was *more* than an inanimate object; it seemed to have a vital energy, a life force of its own. I looked around my small apartment and also saw that my living room chair was not only a "chair." Joyfully, I bounced from room to room: my refrigerator was not merely a "refrigerator"; my dining room window, not simply a "window." I realized that these things were marvels created out of the stuff of the universe and there was an extraordinary bond holding it all together. Fantastic! Living in wonderment is an absolute blast. Living in the absolute is a wonderment.

Truly, the material world is not different from the spiritual. I had been taught this in my journey thus far, but I'd never seen it come to life in such a magnificent way. I felt that everything about me was complete, perfect. Rich with intensity, balanced with innocent simplicity, all things were just as they were—uneclipsed by the limitations of memory. In Zen this is called "suchness," "thusness," or *tathata*.[22]

Because living in suchness and seeing things just as they are is not a selective process, human beings are not excluded. Consequently, I began to see myself for what I really was: a

Each thing just as it is takes on an entirely new significance or worth. Miraculously, everything is radically transformed though remaining just as it is.

—Zen master Yasutani Roshi[23]

selfish, egotistical person who had never really loved anyone. I was in love with the *idea* of my father or my sister or my husband, and those ideas were in my mind rather than truly in my heart. Love for my family was nothing more than self-serving, narrow, and greedy emotion that I had stockpiled in my own precious ego image. I had been taking the love I thought I'd been giving.

Self-denial was one way I thought could atone for my disgraceful behavior. In beginning to confront the most insidious of human complexes—guilt—I played a mind game that went something like this: "If someone in the world is hungry, perhaps my fasting will alleviate their hunger," or "I will not appreciate any material possessions because in the deepest sense of reality no one actually needs them."

As to clothing, that was one thing I surely didn't need more of; so shoes and lingerie were all I could buy whenever I went shopping with Aunt Mac, which was about once a month. I was in atonement on this particular Tuesday, but I kept our date anyway. By evening, my purchases stretched across the bed, I was contemplating their meaning: that red chiffon polka-dot negligee, those brown bikini panties—was I allowing myself to be seduced by the material world, by *things*? And those plaid platform shoes . . . I just wanted to go naked and burn everything I owned! Then I calmed down and decided that I'd bought them and would wear them, but never with joy.

After a series of these attempts to make myself a better person—which included denying myself coffee and tea, candy or sweets of any kind, alcohol (which I rarely drank anyway), and fasting every Monday—I began to see I'd been fooling myself with a ream of rationalizations that meant nothing. That's when I began to understand what self-denial is really all about. True self-denial is denying untruths and willingly giving up precious *notions*—not nightgowns, shoes, treats, or food. True poverty is having nothing *within*.

My focus turned to what was left inside of me; I had to get to the bottom of things in order to be empty. As such, the process of penetrating, probing, and purging the deepest layers of my being was about to begin. At that time, I could not foretell what was to come. But after feeling as if I'd ripped away my skin with my own hands, I came face-to-face with the ugliest, most heinous beast imaginable: me. Shame pierced my being, causing a burning, wrenching pain I could not relieve. It seemed that everything I'd ever done in my life was selfish, wrong, evil, blind—and it all reposed within me. The debt I had created in the universe was unpayable, for it had become the entirety of my selfhood—all that I was.

For many days my tears flowed uncontrollably. When I had no more tears, I cried without tears and red splotches formed around my eyes. I looked like hell and felt like hell. I felt as if I'd been thrown into my own vision, that same abysmal crevasse that echoed cries from other tortured souls, but I'd had no idea what it was really like until I was there. In this place nothing was real: ice was not cold and fire was not hot; light did not shine and dark did not exist; there was no such thing as color, contrast, fragrance, or form. All that existed was a bleak gray fog that wasn't even wet. The problem was, I could see "heaven" all around me, in the everyday world of light and life, the world the way God made it—perfect, ordered, radiant, inseparate from the spiritual world, and, most of all, *real*. But my soul was no longer a part of this world. I wanted to die, yet I knew that even in death I would remain forever in anguish unless I came to understand what I must.

It did not concern me that others lived as I lived—some worse, some better—or that others might trivialize apologies for my transgressions, for in their eyes there may have been none. It was what was in *my* eyes that could not be denied: the *truth*. I could see a powerful and loving magnificence throughout all things—especially in the hearts of human beings—yet my soul was writhing in horror at seeing myself. I was simultaneously in ecstasy and in agony.

Like Ebenezer Scrooge in Dickens's *Christmas Carol*, I was forced to walk through my past relationships and see my actions in the light of reality. Yet I felt what lay ahead would be my darkest night, for something else was happening: I was beginning to die, and I knew it. Even so, physical death was not my main concern. I felt my very soul would be extinguished from the memory of the universe, as if I had never existed. Furthermore, I was actually participating in this process because I was aware of it. In other words, the *me* within was dying.

For a few days I had many

Coming into being is the beginning of destruction and destruction is the beginning of coming into being.

—Hermes Trismegistus[24]

intense thoughts of Jesus' Calgary and crucifixion, yet I did not know where these thoughts came from or why I was having them. I had believed Jesus was a man like any other who truly knew God, as did Buddha, as did anyone else who was enlightened. But as the images of his tribulation appeared across the screen of my mind, I sensed the pain he suffered as he carried the cross— not the physical agony, but the excruciating spiritual wound in seeing those he loved hurting one another. The cross became a symbol of our mortal self, of the burden we all must willingly carry to our annihilation so that we may know eternity. I felt that as Jesus walked to his death, so must I. As he yielded, so must I. As he did this willingly, I prayed I could, too. It is not that I wanted this, I didn't have a choice. I surrendered.

Overcome with a sense of dread before plunging into the darkness, I received solace in knowing others had survived. I was alone, yet there was something within that imparted mo-ment-to-moment courage. We have words in many languages to describe this self-abandoning kind of courage. Although *faith* might pertain, at this point my mental processes were not using many words. I had feelings that could be dragged down to the intellectual level, but somehow their meaningfulness invariably got lost in the descent.

I was able during those few days to reflect on all the inner changes that had occurred in the past six months. It was now early May of 1973, and I realized I had been through quite a psycho-spiritual journey. The intellectual wheel had been tran-scended, and the door to the great unknown had been opened. I was amazed I had known where to go and wondered where I would end up—if anywhere at all. I knew that even if my body survived my impending death, the *person* who survived would never be the same.

I felt so distanced from all I'd known that life itself seemed alien. My words sounded different, breathing was different, sleep was different. I was seeing through the illusion of my old reality and actually experiencing life as never before. I was madly in love with its Creator, deeply in love with humankind, experiencing life to the depths of my soul—and I was dying. How easy it is to give up when life seems dismal and difficult, and how hard when one wants to cling to the splendor of each moment. I was beginning to see love in strangers' eyes, beauty in ugliness, and God's living presence in everything material. I prayed the memory of my visions would live in the universe forever.

I began to understand, with these thoughts and feelings, that I was mourning my own death. I didn't know I had already died until I *thought* of myself. When that happened, one day, my "self" simply was no longer there. When I looked into the mirror of my mind, there was no longer a reflection.

It was morning, still spring in Chicago. Barely one season had passed since my problems had begun, but it seemed like an eternity. I walked through my apartment, and although still a bit groggy from sleep, I was glad to feel the energy of the new day. I began to think about what to wear for work, but soon realized that it was impossible for me to decide because there was no one inside to make a decision. There was just the outside, a shell over which some material would be draped. I had been eradicated.

When my mind cleared, it occurred to me I had not thought of myself since I'd surrendered, about five days ago. I had not even missed my old self until I realized it was gone. My body nevertheless was occupied, and I soon began to see within this body someone who laughed, worked, and played. Who was this person living in my body? I wondered. It was not as if I were an observer to actions taking place within a body previously known as mine. Nor was I a nonparticipant in the life that went on around me. There was no disassociation, but this new "I" was someone I did not know! Whoever had awakened within me as myself, the *awakened* one, had taken over my being. As to the "I" that I had known? Not even a corpse was found.

This dying to your false self is no easy task: raising a corpse to life is child's play compared to it.

—**Meher Baba** [25]

Chapter 3

THE ENCOUNTER

Leftovers, Milquetoast, and the greatest battle never fought . . .

L IFE WENT ON AS NORMALLY AS POSSIBLE, CONSIDERING I DID NOT exist. I remember talking with many of the friends and customers who came into the store to buy or just to chat. Spiritual issues often dominated discussions. I would participate, but my level of participation had changed. There was emptiness inside of me—I was alive and dead simultaneously.

One afternoon, Sergio and I were alone in the store when he began to play his guitar. A veteran of the Vietnam War, Sergio worked for us part time during his transition to a normal life. He was a gentle redheaded Italian, though highly skilled in the martial arts. He never spoke of his tormented past. He just played his guitar when there was nothing else to do.

On this day he was immersed in his music and I watched him. He was alive but I was not—at least not in the way I had been before. I didn't feel disassociated from my actions—I knew I was performing them. Yet there was a shift in the way I perceived them. I had lost the ability to plan because there was no self to consider decisions. Nor was there a self to reflect on actions made. I could recollect my actions, but the recollections were different now: there was no formulation of *me* to place in context with my actions. Basically, the "I" in me had changed, and this "I" would not allow me to do things as before.

In silence I continued to watch Sergio play. He was fully immersed in his music, oblivious to everything else, in pure union with the act. It struck me that this is what enlightenment was all about: living life without concern for anything but the moment— being *in the act*. Yet I knew it was not that simple. Sergio and I were in the same boat: we were both searching souls.

He must have sensed my mood because he asked me what I was thinking. I tried to answer. "Sergio, what you are doing right now is perfection in every way."

"You mean my playing?" he asked.

"No," I replied. "It has to do with the stuff we talk about sometimes, being enlightened and such. Well, you are already doing the very thing I have been searching for." He glanced shyly at me and returned to his music.

I began to wonder if enlightenment was the ability to commune with life and whether I had lost it. Perhaps all of us are already enlightened and don't know it until we lose it by denying the truth of the gift. If this were the case, I wondered, was it too late for me?

I was getting very tired of panhandling in the spiritual realm. I knew I had experienced the death so often referenced in spiritual books. In Christianity it is the prerequisite to being "born again"; in Eastern writings, the precursor to enlightenment. But I certainly didn't feel as if I were in heaven or the state of nirvana. I knew I had experienced an annihilation, yet did not like the way I was compelled to live as a result—in fear of my own spontaneity. I never knew from one moment to the next what I might do.

Although I knew I had under-gone some sort of spiritual trans-formation, I wanted to understand what had happened to me from a psychological perspective. My self-diagnosis was that I'd had an iden-tity crisis and my ego had been de-stroyed. This conclusion made it possible for me to ignore much of what had transpired spiritually and to simply try to find out who was living in my body.

> *The functioning of consciousness takes place spontaneously, and one does not know what will happen. . . . I do not remember something from the past and then act; it is all action in the now.*
> —Sri Nisargadatta Maharaj[1]

I had concluded that Freud's definition of the ego, superego, and id pertained to usual consciousness (centered around an illu-sory self-image), the soul (a learning being), and the unconscious mind (the source of knowledge), respectively—a reductionist in-terpretation. Since I'd had some integration with my unconscious, this had destroyed my ego. Freud wrote, "But, when the ego finds itself in overwhelming danger of a real order which it believes itself unable to overcome by its own strength . . . it sees itself deserted by all the forces of protection and lets itself die."[2] Al-though I knew something unreal could not see itself, be deserted, or let itself die, I felt as if my ego had those capabilities. But while I understood Freud's point, I wondered why he didn't just say, "The ego is not real; it's a phantom, a trick of *thought*." Soon, I pushed aside the psychological explanation as impertinent and superfluous rationale. It was no consolation. I became disgusted, angry, and once again anxious about my lack of understanding.

✠   ✠   ✠

My small apartment had become the private sanctuary where I spent my nonworking time in contemplation, meditation, and prayer. Since my death I had changed my place for the practices of meditation from the living room to the small windowless bedroom—I now preferred lying down rather than the lotus posture. Technically, one is not supposed to meditate in the recumbent position (mostly because it induces sleep), but I found that raising my arms above my head not only allowed for fuller and more even breath, but for *complete* relaxation while awake.

Before going to work each day, I spent about forty-five minutes on my large round bed allowing thoughts to float freely through my mind. There was no need to think them away, or to think them through. Effortlessly, my mind seemed to rearrange itself, and meditation was deeper and more serene. Contemplation was gratifying, for it was beginning to bring answers to my questions. Prayer was more heartfelt than ever before, and yet often it seemed the words and feelings that passed from me to God were scripted by someone else, someone I did not know. Other times, I knew I was conversing with God. On those occasions, I became acutely aware of what was happening on deeper levels of my consciousness. It seemed the more aware I became, the more *un*aware I realized I was. There was a huge empty space inside me that I wanted to fill.

One morning, as I reflected on my journey, ordeal, and helplessness, I realized that if I could find out who I was, I could be normal again. *That* was the understanding I needed and *demanded*. Finding out who I was became suddenly more important than surviving one more moment. I prayed, "Please help me, my God. I do not know who I am and I *must* know. Please tell me who I am!"

But there was silence, a deep silence. In stillness I waited. Then, as if from nowhere, an invisible, powerful force blew away my desperation. Naked and helpless, I sat up on the bed with my arms propped behind me and looked at the ceiling. I had nothing to grasp, not even a question, not even emptiness. Then the words came—emphatically and without equivocation: "It is not *who* you are, it is *what* you are!"

Wow! That's right, I thought, *how ridiculous to be concerned about who I am. Why in the world would anyone want to know something so insignificant?* For a brief moment I was contented, relieved, and pleased to have this wonderful answer, but as logical reasoning returned, I realized it was not an adequate answer at all. Quickly, I turned back to God and inquired, "All right then, what am I?" In the silence I knew that finding the answer would be up to me.

God's answer left me with deeper understanding: knowing *who* we are only perpetuates the illusion of the self-image, the ego. The only way we can we know who we are is by comparing our self to others—knowing who we are *not*, which calls for knowing who everyone else is—and there would not be a bit of truth in any of it. Since ego death, I could no longer perpetuate myself; I'd learned about the illusion. On the one hand, I was glad about this because

You are asking, "Who am I?" and you are not going to get the answer, because the one who will get the answer is false. You may have an idea, a concept, and you think you have found yourself, but it is only a concept; you can never see your Self.

—Sri Nisargadatta Maharaj[3]

I saw the process as fruitless; on the other hand, I experienced a deep sense of loss. It seemed that everyone around me was playing a game I could no longer play—the game of life itself.

Soon, however, my loss became balanced by a refreshing sense of freedom. I began to experience some mental peace and trust in being this person my body carried around. Actually, I had no choice but to trust, since there were not enough thought processes going on to question my actions. Presently I learned that I did not want to do, nor was I going to do, anything to hurt myself or others. At any rate, I felt I had to believe this.

Why was there a self-image to begin with? I questioned. Why do we live under the illusion of a self or ego? Why is this a part of the scenario of creation? The answers to these questions had something to do with the mind's habit of using thought for projection. But why? What was the purpose if it was nothing more than illusion—as futile as applying lipstick or shaving cream to the mirror instead of to one's face.

I was inclined toward the conclusion that ego perpetuation was nothing more than a rude joke played by God on humankind. This joke seemed consistent with Carl Jung's central concept of psychology, the "individuation process," wherein the contents of the unconscious emerge as consciousness.[4] *Why bother?* I wondered.

Any assertion as to what "I am" at the very roots of my being must also be the height of folly.

—Alan Watts[5]

To summarize my journey from usual consciousness, through the subconscious, and into the unconscious: I'd spent the early winter traversing my subconscious; memories I'd filed away as beliefs and the ideas I'd accepted as true had disappeared. Like whispers I could barely hear, the subtle messages from my subconscious had patterned my fears, likes and dislikes, reactions and expectations, and so on. But then I'd *awakened*, only to find I had subjugated myself to an invalid stockpile of information. What I'd been reacting to was not the real world, but the past. It did not exist in the Now. I saw that I had not been living consciously, I had been living *sub*consciously. Only after my awakening, could I recognize the subtle messages from the subconscious and discard them as impertinent. Along with what I discarded went my self-image, my ego.

Now, barely six months later, there was no self. Alive, but not alive, I was awakening in my *unconscious* mind. Like being in a dream while knowing it is a dream, awakening in the unconscious is being awake in everyday life while knowing it is not the only part of existence. One perceives everyday life as an aspect *of* the unconscious rather than separate *from* it.

> *The true unconscious is not unconscious. . . .*
> *The life that you know is simply one of the many areas in which it is conscious.*
>
> *—Seth Speaks*[6]

Having learned to use survival tools while traversing my subconscious, I believed traversing the unconscious would be a similar experience. Not so! Whereas traversing my subconscious seemed as effortless as chewing food— it gave me one thing at a time to ingest, such as a memory, a contention, a habit, a fear—navigating the unconscious was more like having a six-course dinner crammed down my throat at once.

Initially, this was overwhelming. Everything was mixed up

and I couldn't separate one idea from another, one emotion from another. They all came at once, and they kept coming—from what felt like an inexhaustible source, so incomprehensible that I was dwarfed by it. I felt adrift in a stormy sea where each upsurge, having the ability to engulf my entire mental realm, left me desperate to keep my head above water. I *had* to keep afloat to remain conscious—it was a "sink or swim" situation.

Finally, forced to realize that the confusing upsurges from my unconscious didn't require my comprehension *or* my reaction—only my *yielding*—I allowed myself to be moved by the unconscious. And I found that I could remain conscious as long as I didn't resist. I was learning to swim, to *integrate* with the unconscious. In only a few days, this skill improved to the point where I began to feel strong again, more capable of functioning, and more perceptive. As days passed, I was able once again to *think*, but this "thinking" was quite different from my old way of thinking.

This new perception culminated one morning, a week or so after I'd received the message: *It's not* who *you are, it's* what *you are*. I was driving to work, when suddenly I realized I could *see* from another dimension. It seemed that my mind had a body and that body rose above my current mental plane and onto a new plane of existence where life below appeared amazingly clear.

The experience was similar to being thrust into the void, only in this dimension I felt as if I were actually in a *place*. This place was not empty or dark, but was filled with a kind of understanding disassociated from emotion. I couldn't feel much, but I could *think*.

By the time I arrived at work, I could process many

thoughts at a time; instead of one mental eye, a thousand. And yet everything was orderly. Like watching a chess game and immediately knowing how the game could best be played out, I could see life with expanded comprehension. Things came to me all at once, though not intuitively as with my gnosis, but intellectually. I knew I could mentally ascertain and discern anything I wanted to. I had my mind back! And it was in better shape than ever before.

At first, it was so exciting that I didn't care what this new dimension was all about. I could untangle situations that had previously perplexed me, for example, why Joe did this, or Marjorie did that. I could even almost pinpoint where their awareness of their actions left off and subconscious, automatic reactions began. Personalities were before me like a road map, including Pete's. I began to look at him as if he were a child who did whatever he wanted without being mindful of the consequences. When I considered doing the same—perhaps I would just take the day off and hang out somewhere without telling anyone where I was—I realized I was in a very tricky place. My insight was empty of any moral foundation; this new dimension seemed to transcend right and wrong. When I turned to my gnosis for guidance, I could not get in touch with it. I couldn't feel much of anything except unadulterated *power*.

The turbulent waters I'd recently experienced in my unconscious had calmed, for I had integrated with them. The power behind the turbulence and my mind had become one and the same. I could make my own waves if I wanted to, and the temptation to do so was great. Conversely, I felt this power was not just mine alone to use at will—it belonged to everyone. I could not afford to unleash the power at hand—I didn't know what *should* be—yet neither did I know how to contain it.

Moreover, my desires were becoming subtle enough to *change*, chameleon-like, from moment to moment. The strongest of these desires was to restructure my self-image in this new dimension. I was moving perilously toward the treacherous realm of self-inflation. I feared my complete undoing was close at hand.

Once again the tables had been turned. Where the great doubt had crushed my intellect, the new dimension resurrected it. What was old and unreal was now revitalized. I found I wanted to be a part of this intellectual resurrection, but I knew the image created would be unreal. Oddly, the more I denied myself a new identity, the more power I found. Truly, I was in battle with the powers of the *collective unconscious*. (This is a Jungian term, but it is *real*. The collective unconscious is the aggregate consciousness of humankind existing beneath levels of awareness.) I was also in battle with the powers of creation, for just beneath the collective unconscious existed the Source of the power. So thin was the barrier between the two, at times, that I could barely tell the difference.

> *Coming to terms with the collective unconscious in general . . . is* the *great task of the integration process.*
> —Carl Jung[7]

Suddenly, I was caught between reason and acceptance, consciousness and unconsciousness, and the powers of man and those of God. And I *knew* it. Moreover, I was in a new dimension—labeled the "fourth dimension" (a number signifying the abstract) by philosophers and the "fourth plane" by Sufi mystics—where I found myself navigating the most treacherous waters yet.

Swiss philosopher Jean Gebser (1905–1973) wrote about this dimension as exposing one to a "new task" by refusing to indulge the ego's habit of reassembling itself in a "fixity of consciousness." That transcendence is "accomplished only by integration, not by destruction."[8] Even so, a maniacal attitude can develop during integration. According to Jung, when we add universal characteristics of humanity to our consciousness, it brings about inflation; and this inflation can take the form of a "pathological will to power"[9] that can cause a "'splitting of the mind' or 'schizophrenia.'"[10]

Instinctively, I knew that if my ego reassembled itself here, my awareness would be severed from reality. My cord to sanity would be cut, and I would never be able to find it again. But this was not my biggest concern. I was more concerned about the powers in this new dimension, for these powers—I knew beyond doubt—made thoughts come true. I'm not referring to a wish or a dream hoped for, but the immediate manifestation of what one *thinks*.

Sufi mystics delineate spiritual growth into states called "planes," each plane having its own level of awareness. The first three planes include awareness of the three-dimensional world. The fourth plane includes awareness of

We only have to say: "Be," and it is.
    —The Qur'an (16:40)[11]

the real Mind, the universal power that creates the three-dimensional world and beyond. Sufi mystic and teacher Meher Baba describes this plane: "Here the soul is equipped with full power and is even capable of raising the dead and of creating new forms and worlds breathing with life. On the fourth plane there are no occult powers. They are divine powers."[12] And yet, as Meher Baba taught, the overpowering "temptation to wield and use the infinite energy . . . proves a treacherous foe at this juncture. . . ."[13]

Plainly stated, the fourth plane is agonizing; there is no feeling of divinity or godliness about it. The burden of operating from this level of awareness—not knowing right from wrong—is tremendous.

Deathly afraid I would create something heinous or destroy something beautiful without recognizing one thing from the other, I knew I needed to learn some kind of moral sense—not a set standard of dos and don'ts, but a sensitivity that would steer me into deeper understanding of truth. Yet there was no way for me to know what was true, or even if my actions were spiritually accordant, without being able to *feel*. It seemed my heart had been devoured by my mind, which was not interested in feeling. It only wanted to think.

Somehow I knew I could not let my mind take charge of my soul. My intellect was fallible. It had crumbled before, and it could do it again. More importantly, I knew my intellect was capable of lying and leading me into places from which I might not return. I missed my gnosis, my guidance. Most of all, I longed to again feel love for myself and others. I prayed to be able to feel *anything*, even if it was painful.

✢   ✢   ✢

As it turned out, I did not intentionally use the powers of the fourth plane. All my wishes were shared privately with God, as if he were a filter through which my desires needed to pass before entering the world. After a few days, I realized I was again in touch with my gnosis. My prayers had been answered, and I was grateful.

Spring was now in full bloom, and I enjoyed walking down the busy sidewalks near my store. Sometimes I felt as if I were an invisible witness to passersby. But I saw them, their worries and their pain, simply by brushing past them. I wondered why my feelings for others had grown so deep, why I shared their suffering, and why I had no choice about it. The only answer was my boundaries between myself and others had somehow broken down. These occurrences felt similar to the love a parent has for a child.

Somewhere in this period of unfoldment, I began a holistic, or nonsectarian, approach to social concepts and organized religion that remains with me. As I see it, if we believe that *our* religion is the sole, *right* religion and that our hero is the best, or the only, hero, we have succumbed to gimmickry. Religious zealots are myth believers asleep in the unconscious. They have not even begun to integrate with Reality. True spirituality is all inclusive, not separatist.

Huston Smith exemplifies this point with a tale from his book *The World's Religions*.[14] A man goes to the top of a mountain and seizes hold of the Truth. But Satan, suspecting mischief, had directed one of his underlings to follow him. When the demon reported the man's success in attaining the Truth, Satan replied, "Don't worry, I'll tempt him to institutionalize it."

However, it was not this

> *Religion is a defense against the experience of God.*
>
> —Carl Jung[15]

attitude that compelled me to put aside my hero, God. With ego death, or annihilation (which I described in chapter 2), I lost my reflection of self, but found it again in God. *He* reflected me, and without him, I seemed to be nothing. Yet I began to feel that I was limiting God to my reflection of him. I needed to find the *real* God, not a representation or a simulation. In order to do this, I had to let something come into my being, and I could not know beforehand what this would be. If I knew beforehand, it would not be God—it would be a figment of my own imagination. As Sri Nisargadatta Maharaj plainly stated, "In an effort to acquire the good or get rid of the bad, you have invented a God—then you worship such a God . . . and you pray to that God for something good to happen to you."[16]

In opening to the unknown, I once again detected an unrelenting force working to refabricate my demolished ego, but I was getting accustomed to this force by now. I could not accept an ego image, yet this force wanted me to. In looking deeper, I saw that *I* was causing this. It was now time for me to confront my own *will*.

But how does one confront one's own will? Wanting not to want, or willing not to will, or desiring not to desire is as silly as trying to make a hammer hit itself. I needed to understand *why* my will willed for an ego. Since my ego would be nothing more than a neat little package of thoughts with my name on it, this made no sense to me. I had to break the cycle of self-imagery for it was leading me nowhere.

I don't know how it happened, or even what brought me to finally realize I didn't need to have a self. Nor did I need a reflection—even through God—of myself. In fact, I could never *have* a self because I *was* a self! According to Belgian philosopher and Buddhist scholar Robert Linssen, "Tanha, the thirst for 'becoming' is on the point of extinction. The tensions in order to 'become' are replaced by the relaxation of THAT WHICH IS. It is the hour of the 'letting go' of which the Zen Masters speak."[17]

When I realized that my will was nothing more than a "thirst for becoming" and that my thirst for becoming resulted in fear of *non*being instead of simply *being*, I understood I had been excluding reality (the reality of myself—me) by imposing my thirst to *become* on top of what I already was! With this understanding, I felt relieved and grateful that part of my struggle was over. Whew! But I didn't want to delude myself into believing I was enlightened and took no time off from my journey. Besides, I was now invigorated: I wanted to see God more than ever. I began to imagine he might appear at any moment. My heart churned and my soul trembled in anticipation of seeing the Cause of existence, the only real part of me.

> *You are struggling to become something, and that something is a part of yourself. The ideal is your own projection. See how the mind has played a trick upon yourself. . . . When there is awareness of this trick . . . then there is only what is.*
>
> —J. Krishnamurti[18]

Instead, I encountered another force. The darkest, most vile energy came upon me. I felt its frightening and violent power—greater than all the underworld forces I had thus far encountered. It seemed everything negative existing in the entire universe was pressing against my brain, and it wanted in.

The skillful leader subdues the enemy's troops without any fighting. . . . This is the method of attacking by stratagem of using the sheathed sword.

—Sun Tzu[19]

Somehow I knew I would have to face this force, for it would only grow if ignored; and as it grew, fear would grow. As I prayed for protection, I remembered that the concept of *not fighting* had helped in the past. I also remembered that when such forces were confronted, they receded in the light of con-sciousness. Yet I did not want to expose this dark force, for it confused, frightened, and exhausted me. It wanted my power— the power that lies at the deepest parts of all human beings, the power of being conscious in the unconscious, the power to cre-ate, the power to love.

I knew this force had the ability to disguise itself and suck me into wondering what it was—get me to *think* about it. But I could not afford to do that. Nor could I call upon my memory for help when this force was near me. I called upon God, and when I did, all my fears welded into one word: Satan. I also knew this force had many names, which made it even more frightening— for it was not just an image conjured out of anxiety, repression, or guilt by my Christian-trained mind. This force was also known,

The true history of the mind is not preserved in learned volumes but in the living mental organism of everyone.

—Carl Jung[20]

among others, as Namuci (Vedic), Mara (Buddhist), Shaitan (Islamic), and Ahriman (Zoroastrian).

Somehow I had managed to keep this terrifying, heinous force from the forefront of my conscious-ness until one morning. As I was getting ready to go to work, I leaned over the bathroom sink and began to lose balance. I felt perched atop the universe. If I moved even slightly, I was sure to fall directly into hell—for the dark force had returned and was closer to me than ever before.

I looked into the mirror and saw behind my face a black vortex of evil, draining everything into its bottomless abyss. Ignorant, selfish, hungry, and prepared to devour, it watched and waited for me to blink, for my consciousness to lapse, for me to turn away from its presence in denial that it was within me and I within it. Powerless and immobilized, I began to pray as I leaned over the toilet—I was going to throw up. But before I could even get on my knees, everything fell silent. I looked into my mind and realized that a terrible battle had been fought and now it was finished. But why? No answer came. Silence pervaded my inner world.

This silence was not, however, quiet. It was a silence louder than anything I'd ever heard, a silence deafening as all thunder from the beginning of time. This silence existed before sound was conceived and bore the aggregate of all sounds yet to be made. When all sound is heard at once, there is nothing else to hear. Thus it is silent but not quiet.

Again I looked into this great silence and could see that something had opened inside my brain, in the middle of the cerebrum. There was an eye. I perceived it as an eye because I knew that something above, a consciousness, was looking at me through it. I was using this very same opening to see this consciousness and observe the fact I was being seen. One eye, two seers sharing it. In that moment of magnificent silence, it seemed God was looking at me and there was no separation between us but for this eye. God was watching over me, and the calm told me Satan would not enter here.

While trying to remain conscious of the eye opening in my brain, I said a prayer of thanks, finished getting dressed, and went to work. This part of my journey was over. Of this I was assured that same evening.

Thankful my workday had passed with no more unusual experiences, I was exhausted but relieved when I went to bed. As most often happened these days, I was alone. I could confront Satan, but not Pete—not until my journey was over, anyway. I knew I would need firm footing, strength of spirit, and a willingness to face an unknown that was not just in my psyche. And yet since we never argued, I wasn't completely sure if I truly had a marital problem. Perhaps that, too, was in my psyche and my pulling it out might *create* a problem. At any rate, I resolved to do the best I could with what I had at hand. Although I did not always enjoy my solitude, I guess I must have needed it.

It had been barely six months since my journey had begun, and in those months I had learned the importance of pulling my mind and my emotions together without conflict. I lay down on the bed and turned inward to reflect on the day and bring closure to its events. As I did so, lightning began to flash in my brain. Although there was no physical feeling of electric shock, the bursts of light jolted my body. The bolts came quickly, one after another, as if my entire mind were an eye with no eyelid and someone was flashing a powerful strobe light directly at it, again and again. There was no time for thought. I cannot recall precisely the number of flashes, but my best estimate is ten or more. The flashes were accompanied by a tremendous sense of finality. This part of the journey, my gnosis told me, was concluded.

Ah, rest. Sleep came, deep and peaceful . . .

Even though I'd never heard of a photistic experience and was still not relating my journey to the kundalini process, I was not in the least concerned about the lightning flashes in my brain. They had imparted comfort and peace. Dr. Lee Sannella's *Kundalini Experience*, in which he discusses these occurrences, would not be published for another fourteen years. In it he writes, "A variety of photistic (light) experiences may occur during the physio-kundalini process. Some traditions outline whole sequences of such light phenomena."[21]

As to my confrontation with Satan, all I cared about was that I was safe. I didn't even want to understand it, for I had learned it is precisely that effort of understanding dark forces that tricks us into their game! Understanding would later come to me from God himself—the moment I heard, saw, and felt the *word* of creation. I was in a half-conscious state one spring morning, enjoying my haven of silence and darkness before the sun's rising, when something completely unexpected happened. Into my awareness came a word that gushed forth energy, order, action, and manifestation simultaneously. This word was and is the word of creation! What I heard, felt, and saw was a resounding "I"!

In that same moment this word sent forth tremendous energy, and that energy formed order, matter, life, and consciousness. I realized that God manifested creation of himself, but did it in such a way that he did not know it *as* himself. There had to be something else. But since there was nothing else, the word, I, manifested as "Not I." This is the paradox of existence: Creation, including us, is I; but its projection is predicated upon the *illusion* that there is something other than God—something separate, the Not I. This is where humankind's great story begins.

Before the world was created, the Self Alone existed. . . . Then the Self thought: "Let me create the world." He brought forth all the worlds out of himself.
—Aitareya Upanishad[22]

God said, "I," and created the grand illusion that there was something other than himself. This is why we perceive the world as something other than ourselves. If there were nothing outside of, or separate from, our sense of selfhood, there would be nothing to consider as *not* self. We would be all that existed. Similarly, if we did not subconsciously accept the Not I as reality, we would not believe the illusion of creation—we would be unconscious to it. We would be in a primordial state, prior to consciousness in this universe (or any universe) as we know it. Consciousness *means* participating in the illusion. (Enlightenment means knowing about the illusion and still participating.)

The acceptance of Not I as reality is the birth of the ego, which is basically a mental image with which we identify. "I am *this*," however, implies "I am *not that*." Our ego cannot know that I and Not I work in conjunction with each other for the sake of experience. The ego does not see Not I as illusion, for the ego itself is also illusion. Just as a dream remains a dream as long as we sleep, the ego cannot see beyond itself.

So, in the same way God differentiated himself in the universe, we differentiate ourselves from the *massa confusa* (confusing mass—chaos) of creation by distinguishing what we are not. We are then a part of the grand illusion, or, as is known in some Hindu traditions, maya—the illusion that relative and transient existence is absolute Reality.

Illusory things are dependent on Reality itself.

—Hermes Trismegistus[23]

All of creation is a process of the Not I becoming conscious of the I, a living process wherein God is becoming conscious of himself *as* himself. This is a process in which we play a magnificent role, for we are the vehicles through which he accomplishes this miracle. As adept and spiritual teacher Yogi Ramacharaka wrote, "Setting aside first this, and then that, it [the self] finally discards all of the 'Not I,' leaving the Real Self free and delivered from its bondage to its appendages."[24]

Some believe God is total consciousness, never in a becoming state, and does not need us to become conscious of himself. How subtle is the Not I as it rumbles through our minds, separating this from that. And this is the purpose of the Not I, but let's not be fooled by it in the meantime—if God is total consciousness, just whose consciousness is it that learns about God? When we truly open ourselves to the place where, as Japanese Buddhist scholar D. T. Suzuki put it, "God remains God and no process of becoming not-God has yet begun,"[25] we see the process of "becoming not-God" be-

There has never been two from the very first. It was [in] the human act of knowing that God divided himself and became to be conscious of himself as not God and yet God.

—D. T. Suzuki[26]

gin: God forgets who he is so that we may be. There is no greater love than this.

Now, what does any of this have to do with my confrontation with the devil? What does it have to do with why there is evil in the world at all? It has to do with understanding and assimilating fear.

When I saw, heard, felt the word *I*, the universe surged into existence with tremendous force. I can only describe the force as pure emotion combined with purpose of being—in a word, *love*. In Reality, the universe was created, continues to be created, and is maintained by this magnificent force.

But most of us do not live in Reality. We live in the grand illusion. As such, we see things a little backward. In Reality, love has no opposite, for it encompasses all things. It is a creative force, not a destructive force; but this creative force has a by-product that—in illusion—serves to oppose it. This force is the emotion we know as *fear*. Often, instead of feeling love, we fear *not* being loved; instead of *being*, we fear *nonbeing*. Love turned backward is not hate, it is fear.

As I see it, fear is the dynamic that God lovingly provided us at the time of creation to prevent us from being drawn back into the primordial essence of his being. If there were no primal

Self realization must be attained before the unreal can truly be seen as an expression of the Real.

—I. K. Taimni[27]

fear, our consciousness would magnetically return to its great and loving Source—faster than a fly to honey. The problem is, we wouldn't be aware of the Source *or* the love. We would not even be aware of our own existence! Our consciousness would be smaller than an egg on an ovary in our mother's belly. Fear, as a primal force, is simply God's way of pushing us out of the cradle, his "wrong way" sign on a one-way street. The small print at the bottom of this wrong-way sign might read: "For the sake of your own consciousness, do not enter."

As a result, fear often takes a more prominent role in our lives than we would like, or than we even know. Originally, fear was essential to our existence. God wanted us to *be*, and the only way we could be was to fear nonbeing. But we have taken fear to a level beyond its essential purpose, turned it into myth, embodied it, and named it. We have given a force with no consciousness at all—except what we lend it—power. What we perceive as Satan, by *any* name, is merely the aggregate by-product of humankind's fear of nonbeing. All that we have rejected as detrimental to our existence from the beginning of time is still energy. And that energy, or force, resides at a level of consciousness we all share.

In the unconscious, significant concepts are cohesive, embodied almost as entities. Albeit still incomplete, they have been given psychic form by our mass consciousness. Carl Jung called these embodiments "archetypes," meaning characteristics of human nature, or "motives," represented in a psychic form. (It can be a "chicken or the egg" question. Was the archetype created from human characteristics, or vice versa?) Jung wrote that the archetypes reside in the common area of the unconscious mind of all humans, "a mental precondition and a characteristic of the cerebral function."[28] It is only in coming into contact with them *consciously* that they can be seen for what they are: simply characteristics of human nature projected into the field of consciousness.

Until we integrate with our unconscious mind we are limited, chained to an ego that belies truth. We will continue to feel incomplete, make our own idols, and overlay illusion upon perfection. We will live in time without knowing eternity and die without having been born. We will live in fear instead of glory because we will be separate from our Creator—our true Self.

When the illusion is dispelled, fear will no longer stand as a barrier between us and God. We will understand as Jesus: "I proceeded and came forth from God" (John 8:42). We will know, as Yogi Ramacharaka termed it, a state of "Conscious Unity and Identity with the One . . . in the bosom of the Father."[29] Above all, we will solve the riddle of creation: "I and the Father are one" (John 10:30).

In that spring of 1973, I had emerged victorious from my battle with the dark force. At least it had seemed like a battle. In Reality, it was a battle that was never fought. Soon, I would see life in the light of truth. Up to this point in awareness, living in the Now was something I had experienced only sporadically—but I was about to be embraced by eternity . . .

Chapter 4

IMMERSION

Sin and eternity in a bathtub . . .

I T WAS LATE SPRING OF 1973, ALMOST SEVEN MONTHS SINCE MY
journey had begun. The store was approaching its second
anniversary, and Pam, my coworker from Chicago State Hospital, had come to work part time. Arta still managed the bookkeeping while Ricky worked during busy seasons and sales.
Besides Margie and Sergio, we had John and Jimmy—friends who
also helped out—and our two new employees, Jane and Jan.

Some evenings we would sit around and talk—customers
often joined in the conversations—and we never ran out of things
to discuss. Occasionally, friends would drop in to play a new album on the store's stereo system; the music was set up with some
kind of contraption that made the lights on the walls flash in
rhythm.

For a while, Margie had been dating Mick, whose family
owed a chain of tuxedo stores, one of which was down the street
from my shop. Mick was in his early twenties—tall, with black
hair and dark eyes.

On one exceptionally slow evening, Mick came dashing
through the door while I was changing the window display. He
was eager to play his new album, *Jesus Christ Superstar*, so I
stopped to indulge him. But as the overture sounded, my efforts

at polite enthusiasm failed. For reasons unknown, I began to envision three distinct spheres. It was as if there were a painting in my brain that clarified with each passing moment.

I couldn't wait to turn further inward to find out what this was all about. That meant home, meditation, and solitude—things I was guaranteed, for Pete once again would not be there. So I apologized to Mick and closed early.

Over the next two days, the spheres grew closer together. As this happened, I began to recognize my thinking had been linear, as if each thought were a train car, one following the other into the next moment. Then, one evening while Pam and I were restocking shelves at the store, I saw the three spheres fuse into one. Suddenly, all of time was unified into one colossal Now. I could see the past and the future as nothing more than shadows of Now. I was experiencing timelessness, an eternity in which I embraced, loved all things. Eternity showed its face to me as *all* of time—all of time garbed in the emperor's new clothes, moments so fleeting and unimportant that they don't exist in reality.

I understood more clearly how we are deceived by appearances of our own temporal processes, remembering the past and projecting the future without ever living in the present. We fragment eternity into time—even consider it our most valuable commodity—as it boldly moves from moment to moment, taking us along with it, as if we're stuck to the second hand on a clock. Deceived by appearances, we lose focus and forget this temporal process exists

It is in our actual living of eternity that the notion of time is possible.

—D. T. Suzuki[1]

only because of our ability to experience this very moment, the Now.

Now has a place and that place is here. How could Now happen if it did not happen here? Events cannot occur if they are not synchronous with the place in which they occur. There would be no place for the happening to happen.

My sense of living fully in the present was accompanied by the feeling of having arrived. I felt, for the first time, my whole being was *here*, although I did not know exactly where here was. I also knew that wherever I went, it would still be here; in fact, I could not possibly be any other place but here. As I drove home that evening I felt safe being here. As with the Now, here was something no one could take from me. I would soon learn, however, that there was an aspect to being here that I never expected.

During the past months, I had been enjoying long, hot soaks in the bathtub—they were a great tranquilizer. Across the bathroom's ceiling was a beautiful five-paneled antique glass window Pete and I had purchased from an old church. The lighting behind it revealed a phoenix, intricately painted over the colored glass. On a cool night in May, I was to learn the meaning of the phoenix the mythological bird that, after destroying itself in flames, rose from the ashes to experience life anew.

While soaking in the tub this particular evening, I was in a state of repentance. The repentance I knew was not a guilt-filled repentance, however, for I had learned about guilt, which is basically fear of change, and it had lost its hold on me.

Guilt creates and perpetuates an uncomfortable plurality to

our being: our conscience is the good guy, *we* are the bad guy. We want to change the past, we want to change ourselves, and we want to project ourselves into the future as a better person. We want to go back in time and make right the wrong we've committed. When we are in a state of guilt, we want anything but what we have at the moment—yet that moment is the only place where change can occur.

To put it another way, experiencing guilt is like trying to pound a nail but refusing to hit it on the head because we are afraid something might actually change. Instead of undergoing transformation, we choose to wallow in our own humiliation. Rather than change, we indulge ourselves (albeit unhappily) in this psychological complex we have created.

Repentance, on the other hand, is transformation. Where guilt requires memories of the past, repentance requires the here and now. Where guilt stems from ego, which is illusion, repentance stems from the reality of the Self. Where guilt drowns us in circumstantial self-judgment, repentance is emergence of the self from all circumstances. As thirteenth-century Dominican theologian Saint Thomas Aquinas wrote, "The purifying of the soul by the punishment of purgatory is nothing else than the expiation of the guilt that hinders it from obtaining glory."[2]

Most of all, true repentance abolishes the desire for personal transformation. This is the sacrifice we must make in order to rise like a phoenix from the ashes. There is no time for desiring anything in the Now.

As I languished under the phoenix, repenting my heart that spring evening, my soul turned inside out and experienced—on the deepest level—sorrow for having been blind to the beauty and purity of Truth. Filled with remorse, my soul, mind, and even my body were being purged from all things untrue.

Suddenly, I sensed an enormous force around me that had an enheartening calmness about it. It was moving and it wanted to take me with it. In that same instant, I understood that—in reality—*I* had never *done* anything. Neither the person whom I perceived at that moment as myself nor the person I perceived before ego death had ever done anything. Nothing bad, nothing good. Things were done, actions followed, and movement made, but only in a relative, time-bound sense, which I saw as illusion.

I felt I had never gone to school, worked, or gotten married; never cooked a meal, driven a car, read a book, or made a phone call. I had never performed a good deed or an evil one. Most of all, I had never made a mistake, because I had never done *anything*; the "I" in me was removed from all action.

As I sat immersed, a great burden was removed from my soul. There was no reasoning, no questioning, no fear of this force. Lightness filled me and a sense of release abounded. Like a river, powerful yet gentle, this force surrounded my inner being; and as the warm, soft current lovingly engulfed me, I willingly let it. I did not know what would happen next, but I trusted no harm would come to me.

A sense of freedom entered my mind, heart, and every pore of my wet skin. I was totally disconnected from any transgression, any wrongdoing ever committed. This force showed me—not through words, but through a vision that

Actions do not involve Me, nor have I any longing for the fruit of action. He who truly knows Me thus is not bound by actions.

—Bhagavad Gita[3]

imparted understanding—that it was not only I who was free from my actions, but all of humankind as well.

As the experience continued, two atmospheres appeared before me, like gaseous planets with rainbow boundaries that extended beyond my perception. Although I saw only their horizons, it was apparent that one of these atmospheres contained the other, like a sphere within a sphere. I then realized I was in the outer, the larger, of these two atmospheres. (While my soul was in this place, I was fully conscious and aware that my body was still sitting in the bathtub.)

Suddenly, I understood this was the realm where my soul lived, and in this place I had remained untouched by action from the beginning of time. All action somehow occurred in the lower atmosphere, the time-bound one. Just what separated these two atmospheres I did not know. It seemed a marvelous phenomenon. The upper atmosphere somehow ruled or manipulated the lower, without being affected by the lower. Like wind blows sand and neither wind nor sand change in nature, the nature of the upper atmosphere remained untouched and untainted by time.

Then I saw the entirety of humankind there with me, untouchable by deeds of *any* kind. In this experience, I was shown that our minds naturally assume the burden of responsibility for our actions. We punish ourselves—as if we are a closed system of blind autonomy, recirculating the waste matter of the past into today or tomorrow—in hopes of redemption, atonement, or whatever it takes to make us flawless. This force showed me that this closed system is not real; it is a partial truth that our minds have been tricked into accepting as truth. I finally understood the cryptic passage I'd so often heard at funerals: "For now we see through a glass darkly; but then face to face; now I know in part; but then shall I know even as also I am known" (1 Corinthians 13:12).

This force, in making me one with itself, revealed that this universe was created in such a way that *nothing* can compromise the perfection of its nature. It is only our perceptions that are flawed and incomplete; we cannot blemish or defile the perfect source of our being. In truth, we are pure as the essence from which we have been created and always will be, for this part of us is eternal. Therefore, nothing is tainted, and in the deepest sense of reality there is no such thing as "sin." When I saw no sin in me or in anyone else, I redefined sin as a symptom of what we have yet to learn. In other words, we don't need to follow ourselves around, pick up our own trash, take it home, go to bed with it, and hope when we wake up in the morning it will all be gone. It will never be gone because it was never there to begin with. We only *thought* it was.

Does this mean we should sit down and think to ourselves, *I have never really done anything, therefore I'm a good person and have nothing to account for?* No. A convenient state of denial is nothing more than using thought to overcome thought, and that doesn't work either. The realization I'm talking about here calls for first relinquishing control over *all* things we think we've done, not just the ones we choose. And this realization comes via *acceptance*, not denial.

I did not know why I was being shown this, but knowing that there was nothing to forgive felt like the greatest forgiveness anyone

> *The all-pervading Intelligence does not accept the sin or even the merit of anyone. Wisdom is veiled by ignorance. Thereby creatures are deluded.*
>
> —Bhagavad Gita[4]

could ever know. This force did not even seek gratitude, but rather to engulf, carry, teach, and love. Suddenly, I was one with it as it carried me. Yet there was no movement away from anywhere, no movement to anywhere; it moved within itself. At that moment I knew this force to be the same "way" that is written of in Taoism. (Tao means "way," as in the "way of nature.") This experience taught me that the way of the Tao is not the way *to* our true Self, it is the way *of* our true Self.

Lao Tzu is considered to be one of the fathers of Taoism, which began to flourish in China around the time of Confucius (about 600 to 500 B.C.). Historically, Taoism combined with Mahayana Buddhism (Buddhism has origins in Hindu yoga) to form the basis for Zen. Two of the earliest texts from which Taoism is derived are the *I Ching*, which employs divination as a means for understanding, and Lao Tzu's *Tao Te Ching*, which looks to nature as a means for understanding. Both, however, contain the cosmological theory of yin and yang—complementarity of opposites—the foundation of Taoist thought. Yet there is more than one aspect for the practitioner of Taoism to observe, for Taoism is both alchemical and philosophical, as well as a practical way of life.

Most familiar religions have the tendency to dissect God, delineate his characteristics, and describe their functions in an effort to understand him, sometimes as an empirical description. Christianity has the Father, the Son, and the Holy Spirit. Hinduism has the Creator, the Destroyer, and the Maintainer. Even Buddhist tradition has Trikāya (triple body of existence) and bodhisattvas of compassion, war, and so on. Mythology is no different.

The problem with comparing one ideology to another is there is no direct comparison that neatly transposes; they overlap. In other words, it would be inaccurate to equate the Chinese Tao to the Christian Holy Spirit (although I had a tendency to do so, a result of my Christian background). The Tao is not characterized as "holy." Rather the opposite, for it embraces all things and rejects nothing. To call the Tao holy would be to cut its very nature in half. It lives in low places and is exalted in high places. It carries life. In Taoism there are no codified precepts that set religion apart from life with promises of future reward. Living in the "way" *is* the reward.

It has been said the Tao that can be described is not true or complete because the Tao cannot be objectively known. The intellect cannot grasp it because it is that from which reflective abilities spring. To describe the Tao would be like trying to take all words from the beginning of time and spurt them out of one's mouth in one utterance. As a result, the Tao is usually described in similes, which suggest the meaning of an abstraction.

The Taoist sages of China conveyed their experiences from "a recondite realm of mind where the customary divisions of thought do not exist," as Thomas Cleary wrote in his foreword to *Understanding Reality*.[6] In this Taoist alchemical classic written by Chang Po-tuan over nine hundred years

> *In the world there is nothing more submissive and weak than water. Yet for attacking that which is hard and strong nothing can surpass it. This is because there is nothing that can take its place.*
>
> —Lao Tzu[5]

ago, Chang states, "Myriad things are not this, not that; there is not a thing that is not my mind, there is not a thing that is my self."[7] And when Jesus said, "I am the way, the truth, and the life; no one comes to the Father, but by me" (John 14:6), who can dispute he was talking about the Tao—in full identification of himself as *that*, the Tao? One word emerges for one culture, another word for another.

After experiencing the Tao, our mind can move freely without getting lost, because there is nowhere to go but here. And we know that *here*—the manifest world—is the mind. "What is within is also without,"[8] says an alchemical precept from the earliest times (probably prior to 2000 B.C.). The ancient alchemists, according to Carl Jung, sat on the bridge that "unites psychic and material events in one."[9] The mysteries of the universe unfold not from some alien place but from within the manifest world. This is the basis of Taoism and why it has, over the centuries, adopted an alchemical aspect: the physical world is an intrinsic part of *us* as well as an expression of the ultimate order of all things.

As I sat in the bathtub that evening, I was detached from my personal involvement in life, but I did not feel alone. Somehow my disassociation was balanced by complete association with the truth as I saw it. That truth was that everyone else was in the same boat with me; no other human being had ever done anything either. It all happened and happens in the Tao, and we just *think* we are doing all this. I understood that we have been believing the *appearance*, excluding the reality. I felt as if I'd returned to (in biblical terminology) the Garden of Eden. In Zen and Taoism this stage of awareness is considered a natural "nonaction" or "path of nondoing," also known as *wu-wei*.

Just as eternity is all of *time*, the Tao is all of *action* from the be-

The way never acts yet nothing is left undone.
—**Lao Tzu**[10]

ginning of time within that eternity. In containing action, the Tao protects the most precious—innocent, untouched, and eternal—part of every human being from the effect of those actions. In Zen, this eternal part of us is known as the "unborn," or the "face before you were born." Basically, it is our essential self, the soul.

Because the Tao is one with eternity, the orderly expression of eternity—time—can exist with action, and we can have an event. There would be neither time nor motion were it not for the Tao. "Into eternity all movements of time go back," said Hermes Trismegistus, "and from eternity all movements of time take their beginning."[11]

Simply put, time recycles itself. And yet we tag ourselves to each moment as if it will pull us into eternity without realizing the moment itself *is* eternity. Until we experience the finite as an expression of the infinite, we will not know that the only way we can experience eternity is through time—and the only time that exists is the present. "Nothing exists of time," according to Saint Thomas Aquinas, "except *now*."[12] And as American mythologist and folklorist Joseph Campbell commented, "Eternity isn't some later time. Eternity isn't even a long time. . . . Eternity is that dimension of here and now that all thinking in temporal terms cuts off. And if you don't get it here, you won't get it anywhere. . . . this moment of your life is actually a moment of eternity."[13]

Experiencing eternity reveals the truth that *our conscious-*

ness turns eternity into time. According to D. T. Suzuki, "It is only when our unconscious consciousness or what might be called super-consciousness comes to itself, is awakened to itself, that our eyes open to the timelessness of the present in which and from which divisible time unfolds itself and reveals its true nature."[14]

What Suzuki terms "divisible time," I call (in the tradition of Zen master Dogen) "individual time." Because individual time is our personal sense of orientation with the world around us, it is connected to thought and memory; thus it coordinates with our actions in general. However, all of this takes place *within* eternity. Eternity is not divisible, but it appears to be so through our individual experiences.

Japanese Zen master Dogen (1200–1253), historically regarded as a brilliant teacher, declared in his famous essay "Being Time" that we actually *are* time itself:

> *Self is arrayed as the whole world. You should perceive that each point, each thing of this* whole world *is an individual* time. *The mutual noninterference of things is like the mutual noninterference of* times. *For this reason there is* arousal of minds at the same time, *there is* arousal of times in the same mind. *Cultivating practice and achieving enlightenment are also like this. Arraying self, self sees this—such is the principle of* self *being* time. . . . *There must be* time *in oneself. Since oneself exists,* time *cannot leave.*[15]

Dogen's concept of being time is difficult, if not impossible, to intellectualize because time cannot be objectively removed from our self. Dogen's statement, however confusing, does correlate (a bit more comprehensibly) with the following by Albert Einstein:

An important property of our sense experiences, and, more generally, of all of our experiences, is their temporal order. This kind of order leads to the mental conception of a subjective time, an ordering scheme for our experience. The subjective time leads then via the concept of the bodily object and of space to the concept of objective time . . . [because we] coordinate to it [the bodily object] an existence, independent of (subjective) time, and independent of the fact that it is perceived by our senses. We do this in spite of the fact that we perceive temporal alterations in it.[16]

Einstein's "temporal order" is Suzuki's divisible time and Dogen's individual time. According to Einstein, the subjectivity of our ordered experiences leads us to believe time can be objectified as a concept separate from ourselves, when it cannot. What is objectified is only temporal *memory* of order. So, Dogen, Suzuki, and Einstein all agree we cannot remove time from ourself because it is a part of us. Time is nature's order of eternity, a finite expression of the infinite. And yet, as contemporary physicist David Bohm clearly stated, "Thought has entangled the brain in time."[17]

To understand our involvement with time from a psychospiritual standpoint we must transcend it. Forgiveness and repentance have nothing to do with any religion, any belief, any ideas filed away as pertinent. It is much simpler than that. Repentance is *accepting the finite* and forgiveness is *accepting the*

God and eternity then are the first principles of all things which exist.

—**Hermes Trismegistus**[18]

infinite. The very act of this acceptance is God himself, embracing and being embraced.

After the experience in the bathtub that evening, I rose from the ashes of my past and decided everyone else should, too. I ordered myself some spaghetti with meatballs, put on my red polka-dot negligee, turned on the television, and waited for Pete to come home. I had been forgiven all my transgressions and thought so should he. But I guess Pete forgot where *here* was because I didn't see him until dawn.

✤   ✤   ✤

By late May, nearly seven months into my journey, my life had settled subtly into a new phase. My daily routine had not changed dramatically. The store was still doing well, as was my family. However, the emotional drain from my marriage was subsiding, for I had now accepted Pete's alienation as a part of my spiritual journey—a journey wherein progress is fueled not by frustration or anger, but by *understanding.*

As I turned further inward, I began to have mystical insights, one after another. I considered keeping a journal of these occurrences so I could remind myself or tell others of the wondrous things I was learning—but there seemed to be no time, because almost everything was becoming mystical.

Simple activities brought deeper understanding of how the mind works. Shadows cast by objects showed me how we eclipse our own sense of selfhood. Mistaking a semblance on a wall for the object that shapes it is similar to how we sometimes mistake our effect on the world for our self. We also forget that there would be no shadow without a light source and a background—our light source is consciousness and our background is creation. Patterns also took on significance: the design between words on the page of a book or newspaper often became more interesting than the words themselves—I saw space between objects as integral to their existence, part of them.

Motion, as well, intrigued me. I was amazed at how something could be in one spot at one moment and another the next; I wondered what effect that had on the world. A falling leaf, a bird flying overhead, or a car zooming past changes the spacial arrangement of all things. I was both surprised and sad to realize how easy it is to take for granted everyday happenings, as if they are nothing special at all. The human mind is a marvel, yet it gets entangled in its own environment to the degree it cannot see life as alive and ever changing—new each moment—all for the sake of our existence.

With each experience, I tried to learn something, but after a while I began to see the physical world as the mystical world. Ultimately, I realized, there is no such thing as a mystical experience—*everything* is mystical.

My experiences were reality to me because they *exposed* reality—a greater and deeper and more encompassing reality—the principles by which this universe was/is made.

> *Enlightenment consists in spiritually elucidating facts of experience and not in denying or abnegating them.*
>
> —D. T. Suzuki[19]

Thus these experiences were also reality for everyone else, too, even if they didn't know it. It was not just my illusory, separate self that was one with the Truth—*everyone* was. To have believed otherwise would have been like thinking the sun shines on only a few people. It was impossible for me to understand on a level other than the all-encompassing and universal.

Although gnostic knowledge derives from experience only, I was grateful for having read, over the years, about many philosophies, religions, and ways of life because my next experience was to be one that combined the physical world with the spiritual with shocking impact. During an afternoon of meditation, I began to notice a physical sensation in my forehead, as if someone, or something, was lightly touching the center of it. At first it was like the tickling of a feather, then like firm pressure from a fingertip. The sensations grew stronger with each passing day and each meditation. Within a week I began to feel this spot move involuntarily—as if there were a little spastic muscle in the middle of my forehead—when I was working, walking, or driving. Surprising experiences as a result of some inner transformation had become less alien to me, and I was about to have an astonishing surprise one Wednesday afternoon in early June of 1973.

I was busy with a customer who had just gone into the dressing room when, suddenly and for no apparent reason, I felt an opening in the middle of my forehead. The next thing I knew, I could see through this aperture. It was an *eye*! I could feel the lid open and close more surely than in my own two physical eyes. This was the "third eye" I'd read about in my studies of Eastern spiritual practices, and it was now open. Unlike the opening in the center of my brain—the eye of God looking at me—this was different: I could see the physical world through this eye. Slowly it opened and closed, but not in synchronization with my other two eyes; it had its own tempo.

I ran to a mirror to see what it looked like before anyone else did. I had inferred that it would appear about twice as large as my other two eyes. To my relief, it didn't reflect in the mirror. It could be seen *through*, but it couldn't be seen. I was puzzled as to how something could feel so physical and actually *function*, yet not be reflected in the mirror. Then I closed my other two eyes and saw darkness, but my third eye could visualize everything in the external world so normal sight was not needed, just as we do not need to see music to experience it. When I reopened my physical eyes, my third eye saw the world around me as well. In fact, when my third eye was open my physical eyes seemed unnecessary.

But third eye open or not, I still had to carry on as usual. I closed the store and went to have dinner with my friend Mary. I was tired from a long day's work, but I looked forward to seeing her. I hadn't told Mary about my inner life or about my third eye being open. As I watched her through my third eye cooking dinner in her little kitchen, suddenly I was overwhelmed by the sense that she was as close to me as I was to myself—that truly, we are all on this planet as sisters and brothers, spawned from and loved by the same Great Being. But had I confided this to Mary, the next thing I probably would have told her about was the day I became a T-bone steak, that Now is the only reality, that there is no difference between the material world and the spiritual—and "Oh, yes, I have just grown an invisible eye!"

Part of me wanted desperately to share my experiences with others, but I knew how silly I would have sounded. I felt like a student whose teacher would not allow discussion outside the classroom. I was in no position to intellectualize or defend what I was learning. I could only accept what was happening in silence and pray I would integrate my experiences while appearing normal to the world around me.

Mary and I ate dinner—a wonderful dish of Italian sausage with red sauce and spaghetti—and talked about her plans to move to a larger apartment. At evening's end, she gave no indication that anything about me was strange or changed. But I knew differently.

I had often read Eastern philosophy and seen art that depicted an enlightened individual as having a third eye, yet I was still personally ignorant about enlightenment. I'd always thought of a third eye as something spiritual, or beyond the physical. Even though I had sporadically experienced the physical world as *being* the spiritual world, I still believed the spiritual world was complete unto itself and that the physical world was merely a part of spirit life and should not involve the opening of the third eye. But I now had a third eye through which I could see, so I knew I still had much to learn.

> *No doubt the third eye is opened by operation, but this operation can never be performed in hospitals. For this operation you need a living area full of spiritual atmosphere. . . . In this operation our surgeon is . . . eternal mind.*
> —Rammurti S. Mishra[20]

At first, the eye in the middle of my forehead had an eyelid that opened and closed of its own accord, but after a couple of days I learned some control over it and the lid seemed to disappear. When my third eye had opened involuntarily, I'd felt no difference in my inner being. However, when I consciously opened it (and I could do this by just thinking about it), I felt my being rise and condense into that one spot—as if my consciousness had become a physical entity located in the middle of my forehead.

Because I had read that the opening of the third eye was supposed to happen only to an enlightened one, I was puzzled—I had no sense of being the least bit enlightened and thought there should be more to it. I decided to ask internal questions in hopes the answers would come to me, perhaps from my guides or perhaps from God—questions about the why and wherefore of things, questions about the operation of the universe, questions about the nature of humankind. It seemed that no matter what I was doing during waking hours, I was buzzing around in a constant state of internal inquiry. I wanted to know everything.

As my soul asked questions, answers came. But the gnostic process had changed for me. Before the opening of my third eye I had perceived information as coming from somewhere outside myself. Since the opening of the third eye, I could see that the source of information was not from *outside* myself, but *from* myself. The conversation with the Self had begun.

> *Truly there is in this world nothing so purifying as knowledge; he who is perfected in Yoga, of himself in time finds this within himself.*
> —Bhagavad Gita[21]

It was an amazing process to watch: as questions arose, *I* answered them. The format, however, was not the usual query-and-response sequence. The questions themselves were transformed into information, without any separation. In other words, my mind would wonder about something and the very wonderment itself became the response by reforming the question. This changed my perspective, and I was able to comprehend the answer by looking directly at it.

Usually, when asking such a question as, What day is it today? we look to our memory for context, What day was yesterday? What did I do then? Out of this we eventually squeeze a conclusion. We think we have gotten an answer and it's the right one: "Yes, today is Tuesday." We feel a sense of place and time in this process of intellection; this is because of context. Yet whenever there is context, we are looking at something that is *not* the answer, only what surrounds it.

The process I was experiencing was quite different: answers sprung directly from the question, without context or intellection. The very *thing* was before my consciousness immediately as the question was posed. When I asked myself, for example, "Why are we here?" the answer was, "Because you *are* here." And *here* was opened before my eyes as truth—the answer already existed in the question. When I asked, "What makes the difference between individual will and universal will?" the answer came as "What you *will*," and my mind was molded into seeing that my will was the same as Universal Will. I could see the direct, inherent answer, though not by a usual pattern of distilling, eliminating, or deducing. I came to see that answers were everywhere, that Truth needs no contextual affirmation; it is complete unto itself. This is where every truth points directly to the only real truth—the Absolute. In Zen this is called "direct seeing."

The third eye is the beacon to the inner universe that sees the inner and outer as inseparable. This eye sees all of creation as unified and yet permits one to operate within the world of complexities and multitudes. The opening of the third eye is the opening of knowledge, which is understanding and experiencing—in unison—life's phenomena. When the third eye opens, the intellect and the emotions, thoughts and feelings, can finally work together—as one.

The opening of the third eye is the pure and simple cognitive ability to see living Truth, unfettered and pure. Truth is not something we can put our finger on or file away as real or pertinent. It cannot even be written or talked about with any accuracy, for words are only pointers. The most amazing thing about the opening of the third eye is that it sees Truth as *alive*. Untouched by human intellect, unstirred by emotion, and undivided in its purpose, Truth is the living principle upon which the universe was and is created.

> *The third eye is representative of eternal knowledge. . . .*
> —**Rammurti S. Mishra**[22]

Something else began to happen with the opening of my third eye (the $\bar{a}jn\bar{a}$, or brow chakra). I began to feel sensations in my crown chakra, on the top of my head. This last chakra, which I call the "top chakra," is so complex that in some yoga systems it is not believed to be a mere chakra. This chakra allows for the unification of the Absolute with human consciousness. Through this chakra I was soon to have grandest experience of all: "Electrifying Oneness" with the universe. Before the Electrifying Oneness, however, I would experience what the Christian mystics call the "beatific vision"[23]

—only I call it the "beautific" vision—and traverse the levels of creation.

✧   ✧   ✧

It was nearly mid-June and a week or so had passed since the opening of my third eye. As I was leaving my apartment house on this particular morning, I looked toward the sun filtering through the clouds and became transfixed. The earthly scent of the night was lingering in the air, filling my lungs. Within that breath, I heard these words: "The secrets of the universe are not secret. That is the secret!" I looked about and everything seemed transformed into an incredibly marvelous creation, and I realized that I had not been seeing it!

Everything was in its proper place with no improvements needed. The world was perfect. I was mesmerized by the magnificent song of a bird, the movement of the wind through the trees, and the brilliance of the sun, which shone on nothing other than heaven. *Why am I being shown this?* I wondered, and the answer came: "Because it is the truth. Heaven is no place but *here*." I wanted to go back inside and reexit, so I might once again hear those words. But I was late in opening the store. As I left, the words stayed with me.

With each passing day I saw more clearly the sublime symmetry and perfection in all things. And behind all things, I saw a living Consciousness, which I called "God" or "my Father," and communication with him became constant as breath. There seemed to be love everywhere, radiating from everything—a love I'd never known before. All of creation loved me, and I loved all of creation.

Nothing could compare to the luminescence of dust on my windowsill or the intricate movements of a beetle as it scampered through the grass. I was humbled by the sublime beauty of this world and enraptured by the resplendence God was sharing with me. I could see love flowing *to* all things, *from* all things, and *in* all things.

> *All things are per-ceived in the light of charity, and hence under the aspect of beauty: for beauty is simply Reality seen with the eyes of love.*
> —Evelyn Underhill[24]

The power of this love is beyond description. It wipes away every problem, every doubt, and shows that complete and total bliss is the way humankind is truly meant to live. This love cannot be touched by anything imperfect, for it makes all things perfect. This love is our legacy from our Creator—a gift *and* a right. It is God's eternal and unbroken bond with us.

I was totally immersed in the blissful present, where I observed the magnificent order of the universe, where everything worked with no opposition or conflict. Within and without were no longer separate. Everything material emanated pure and simple truth, and everything unseen emanated pure and simple innocence. Not only did all things come from truth, they *were* truth. The spiritual world and the material were one. I knew, more surely than anything, that I was connected to the Source of creation. Every truth I had learned through the gnostic process suddenly cohered into one great living truth: the Truth of God. A yearning to be closer to the Source pulled me deeper into the magnificent order of creation. I desperately wanted to see God, but instead there was a hint of a great mathematician.

All things began in order . . . according to the ordainer of order and the mystical mathematics of the city of heaven.

—Sir Thomas Browne[25]

As I observed the universe around me, I saw numbers and meticulous geometrical arrangements that evidently followed the direction of a living consciousness, a will. Since I am not skilled in higher mathematics, the experience was like peering through a veil. I could see what was there but found it difficult to define. I wondered if our great mathematicians and physicists had this same experience—if true genius was simply being open to, accepting, and ascertaining the significance of what was right in front of one's nose.

Everything was stripped of its guise and revealed as originating from the One Great Living Source that pervades all things, seen and unseen, physical and spiritual, all potential, all energy. I saw everything as the true One. I was madly in love with it and had never felt more secure or more joyous in my life.

Drunk with the brew of God's omnipotence, I was beginning to believe this was enlightenment. There was nothing more I wanted or needed, for I felt I was living in heaven. This was all I had ever wanted, and to see it come true, actualized in such a magnificent way, filled me with gratitude and love. Fulfilled, at peace, and experiencing truth in the words "The kingdom of God is in the midst of you" (Luke 20:21), I was *home*.

The mistake consists in our splitting into two what is really and absolutely one.

—D. T. Suzuki[26]

I had found my joy and it was God. He filled me with a love no human being could match. I saw that I had been unfair to my family, even Pete, in expecting too much from them. Now I was fulfilled, and there was nothing else to ask for, except to share with my fellow humans the legacy of God's love. But I had no intention of going around sharing the "good news" or being evangelistic in any way. Nor would I—except to share with others their beliefs—discuss matters of God. It was all but impossible for me to say the word *God*, for I knew he had different names in different religions.

I also knew the "beautific" vision was not merely a Christian phenomenon, but elemental in any tradition that validates the wonder of creation as well as the ability of human beings to experience it in its glory. We may translate the experience into the language of our particular religion or culture, but whether we are Christian, Buddhist, Hindu, Native American, Islamic, Judaic, Taoist, or Sufi, the experience is the same.

According to scientist, author, and Jesuit priest Pierre Teilhard de Chardin, if God cannot be seen first in all things, he cannot be seen at all. He wrote, "The soul can only rejoin God after having traversed *a specific path* through matter—which path can be seen as the distance which separates, but it can also be seen as the road which links."[27]

Evelyn Underhill characterized this "illuminated vision of the world" as follows:

> *Closely connected with the sense of the "Presence of God"*
> *. . . the vision of "a new heaven and a new earth" . . .*
> *takes, as a rule, the form of an enhanced mental lucid-*
> *ity—an abnormal sharpening of the senses—whereby*

an ineffable radiance, a beauty and a reality never before suspected, are perceived by a sort of clairvoyance shining in the meanest things.[28]

She also explained that "those who will listen and be receptive will find themselves repaid by a strange sense of extended life, an exhilarating consciousness of truth. . . . The heart outstrips the clumsy senses and sees . . . an undistorted and more veritable world."[29]

"Ah, *there* is God!" was the revelation slapping my mind, heart, and soul with every sight in the beautific vision. In this state of openness to Reality, I began to understand the difference between believing in God and seeing God. In this beautific vision the face of God was not just *in* all things, the face of God *was* all things—alive, loving, and omnipotent beyond comprehension.

Having seen *myself* in matter as matter and now seeing *God* in matter as matter, I finally understood the human tendency to personify God and deify matter. I had apprehended God in matter and knew I was surrounded by his majesty, but I wanted him closer to me than that. Perhaps this is because I was yet to see him in myself. Teilhard de Chardin's following prayer is an example of this:

Matter, you in whom I find both seduction and strength . . . I surrender myself to your mighty layers. . . . Let your attractions lead me forward, let your sap be the food that nourishes me; let your resistance give me toughness; let your robberies and inroads give me freedom. And finally, let your whole being lead me towards Godhead.[30]

God exists both in the material world and above and beyond his creation. He is intrinsically connected with and actively living within this universe as an expression of himself. One who has experienced the beautific vision cannot see otherwise; there is no disdain for matter and no perception that it is mundane or dead. There is no need to separate God from his creation and look for him elsewhere. There is nowhere to look except deeper into the place where he's been seen most clearly. In the beautific vision, that place is the manifest world.

In the Sufi delineations of the planes of awareness, I had at this stage surpassed the difficult and dangerous fourth level (see chapter 3) and was somewhere between the fifth and sixth planes. As I said earlier (and my definitions are grossly overgeneralized), the first three planes represent the world as we know it, and the fourth plane is where the creational powers of the universe exist. Continuing on, the fifth plane is mind (conscious, subconscious, and some of the unconscious contents), the sixth plane is emotion, and the seventh plane is Reality. This last is where conscious union with God takes place. Thus the seventh plane incorporates varying states of godhood and is the realm of those whom we might recognize as saviors: Buddha, Jesus, Muhammad.

Sufi master Meher Baba taught that "in the sixth plane of consciousness, the mind itself becomes the Inner Eye and sees God."[31] He believed, "This loving of God and the longing for His union is really and fully demonstrated in the sixth place of consciousness. Only when the sixth plane of the mental sphere is transcended, does Illusion vanish with the vanishing of the last trace of impressions and Reality is realized."[32]

In Sufi belief there is only one Reality, and that is God. To the Sufi mystics, in the deepest sense, that is all there is. Reality is not experienced until one has conscious union with God. This takes place on the seventh (and final) plane.

✧   ✧   ✧

Little more than a week after the onset of the beautific vision, it began to fade. Part of me wanted desperately to cling to it. Yet a greater part of me wanted to be even closer to the One who made such beauty, and I knew I could not do this if I were stuck in the vision. So, like a child who wanders into the dark, I left perfection and bliss behind, perhaps without quite knowing it.

Afterward, like a faint melody or a lover's passing embrace, it haunted me. The pulse of the universe had become my heartbeat. But the bliss of heaven vanished from my consciousness like seafoam dissolving in a receding tide. There was another journey ahead, a journey in which the levels of creation would open before my eyes, and I would learn how the world creates itself through our very consciousness.

And the first Mind . . . which is Life and Light . . . gave birth to another Mind, a Maker of things. . . .
—**Hermes Trismegistus**[33]

Chapter 5

THE WORLDS

The order of chaos and the wisdom of flowers . . .

ONDERMENT AT THE MAJESTY OF THE UNIVERSE from the sanctuary of God's loving arms had receded from my consciousness. My soul had slowly emptied of things comforting and familiar. It was still June of 1973; barely two seasons had passed since my journey into the unknown began. I wondered when it would end or whether I was on a spiral to nowhere. Although I was grateful I'd been shown many things about human nature, God's nature, and the nature of the universe, I was once again in a state of uncertainty. As the beautific vision faded, I became insecure. While I would soon learn that there can be profound wisdom in insecurity—the sort of wisdom that spurs growth—I would also learn, as Tibetan teacher Tarthang Tulku wrote, that "Knowing and Being enter into a partnership in which knowing and knower are the same."[1]

On an everyday basis, I was functioning as well as ever. But having lost the recent bliss of the beautific vision, I was again torn between the conscious and the unconscious, between fear of the unknown and my love for God. I was afraid to go further into the unknown but knew I must in order to know God more fully. My inner and outer life had become almost indistinguishable. And this confusion, combined with a desire to finish my journey, led me to places I'd never imagined existed. I began to traverse new territories—new territories that appeared to me as "worlds."

The first world presented to me was one of conflicting opposites. I began to notice that every time I thought of one thing, simultaneously its opposite would emerge. If I thought of something quite pleasurable, something quite as painful would enter my mind. If I wished for one particular thing to happen—for instance, happiness for a friend in her upcoming marriage—the vision of the opposite—in this case, disappointment and hurt—would appear. In recognition of this, I was compelled to consciously dispel the unwanted vision. The problem then was that the desired vision would also leave. Since I could see no purpose in this mysterious popping up and disappearing of opposites, I concluded I was at a new level of awareness, one that I labeled the "world of opposites."

Nothing could enter my mind without the upsurge of its counterpoint. Soon choosing or even expressing likes and dislikes became futile. For every flower, a weed; for every laugh, a tear. When this is experienced in one's own mind *as* one's own mind, desire cannot be satisfied. Wanting anything is pointless.

In the world of opposites, the unexpected comes along with the expected. As such, my anticipation of continued despondency became balanced with a bit of fun, and I came to understand that everything in the world is a result of this process. When theosophist H. P. Blavatsky wrote of "two opposing elements . . . being necessary to each other for a common object: that of procreation,"[2] she was not just talking about making babies. She was talking about the creational process of the entire universe.

I watched in amazement as my mind called upon one idea at the same time as its opposite—the rising and falling, creating and destroying all took place at once. I felt as if someone had given me a toy that ran by itself.

In due course, I began to see the opposites as nothing more than polarities. For one thing to exist, there must be something *other* that is directly related—hot and cold, light and dark, up and down, and so on. This was all simple enough to understand, and I knew from physics that in order to observe an object in motion, there must be a reference point, for motion implies at least some form of no motion.

You are being taught, and you are teaching yourselves to handle energy, to become conscious cocreators with All That Is, and one of the "stages of development" or learning processes includes dealing with opposites as realities.
—Seth Speaks[3]

This perception was not, however, easily dismissed as elementary physics once my consciousness had merged with the process itself. When so merged, the laws of physics seem only a manifestation of God as he operates through the human mind. The most cogent observations our scientists make seem only beautiful whispers in the wind compared to their source—the universal Mind. I was elated to realize there was a Mind that, unlike my human mind, would never deteriorate—a Mind that was eternal and all encompassing, a Mind that was willing to share its dynamics of creation with me. This Mind, to me, was the "mental body" of God—not his entire being, but the principles by which he created and operated within the universe.

I was coming to understand that opposites, being connected, affect each other; action upon one end of a pole causes a response down or up on the other. This polarity is not outside of the mind; rather, it is a dynamic *of* the mind. Yet we resist the process. We want *this* and not *that*, without realizing that *this* cannot precipitate into our lives as a reality without a little of *that*. When we are conscious of polarity, *this* can finally exist without so much work. When we no longer resist the opposite of what we want, we get what we want. As physicist and author Fritjof Capra declared in *The Tao of Physics*, "Whenever you want to achieve anything, they [the Taoists] said, you should start with its opposite. . . . On the other hand, whenever you want to retain anything, you should admit in it something of its opposite. . . . This is the way of life of the sage who has reached a higher point of view. . . ."[4]

Somewhere between my encounters with the world of opposites and those of the next world I would enter, I recognized I had been branded, marked. I couldn't see it, but I could feel some kind of insignia on my soul. In comparing the location to my physical body, it would have been in an area between my heart and throat, in the middle of my sternum. This branding was neither positive nor negative. I neither liked nor disliked it, and it had no effect on me except to serve as a symbol of what had already transpired in my journey. I knew I was marked because of my experiences, which would continue whether I wanted them to or not. Wanting and not wanting had become the same thing.

The insights I'd received since the previous November seemed a rising spiral to eternity, carrying my soul farther along, inward and outward at the same time. The world of opposites then changed, before my eyes, into the "world of complements."

The world of complements more deeply affirmed there was no completeness in any concept unless the other half (which is the other end of the pole) was simultaneously spawned. Yet in the world of complements there were no opposites; one idea was related to the other without opposing it. What a sense of freedom this brought. What a life I would have with absolutely no conflict, no opposition! I finally realized, as Teilhard de Chardin wrote, "The fires of hell and the fires of heaven are not two different forces, but contrary manifestations of the same energy."[5]

Opposites are complementary.
—Physicist Niels Bohr[6]

The world of complements is the world of opposites as seen from a more holistic perspective. But I wondered, If opposites are not really opposites, why the charade? What's the dynamic involved in the *apparent* opposition? My questions were soon to be answered with a vision—I would be shown how the human mind is the medium for the building blocks of matter. The material world is not so material; it is made up of energy contained in ideas that have cohered into a denser mass and form than we would normally perceive as thought. Nevertheless, it is still thought.

It was still June when I awoke to a symphony of bird songs outside my kitchen. Grateful for such a grand welcome to a new day, I arose and peered through the window at the cloudless morning sky. To my surprise, I saw the world outside in two ways. The trees and the sky were upside down and right side up simultaneously, like a reflection in a still lake. When I tried to understand what was happening, my mind *became* the very thing I was seeing. Inside my head were the sky and trees I'd just seen outside the window. My mind—now sky and trees—was split into two horizontally juxtaposed parts, upper and lower, just as was the initial vision outside.

In looking closer, I could see that the upper and lower parts of my mind were not identical. Each part only contained *partial* ideas whose complement existed in the other half. Bound to each other, as if they were connected by an invisible cord, these half-ideas remained separate, yet sympathetic. Each half needed the other to manifest.

These partial ideas then began to move, and a magnificent combination took place. They gravitated toward each other like threads falling from heaven and rising from earth, winding around each other and weaving a tapestry of completeness as they combined in the dimension of space and time.

Since all opposites are interdependent, their conflict can never result in the total victory of one side, but will always be a manifestation of the interplay between the two sides.

—Fritjof Capra[7]

With this vision, I understood that opposites—complementary parts of one idea—are incomplete concepts that *nurture* each other until maturity. The invisible cord that connects the complements, like a "connection of incompleteness," directs their exchange of energy in a way I can only describe as magnetically gravitational. This connection of incompleteness is the pole of perceived opposites, but it is not an inert straight line; it is moving and alive with energy. This process occurs every moment, over and over, with everything we touch, see, hear, smell, or taste. In the world around us—at *this* very moment—this process is going on in the deep recesses of our minds, which is the Mind of the universe. God procreates, we cocreate.

✣ ✣ ✣

When I experienced the world of complements, I was simply glad to be rid of the opposites. After traversing the world of complements, I was glad to be finished with that one, too. I lived in hopes of seeing some finality, some conclusion to my understanding, but everything still kept changing. I was now grateful for the stability I found in my work and in my (albeit imperfect) home life. As long as those two arenas didn't alter drastically, I believed I could manage my metamorphosis without being overwhelmed in the process.

So opposites became complements, which became the next world. Although I would spend anywhere from a few days to almost two weeks in one world, it seemed I was out of one world and into another before I knew it. Like a breath to which we cannot cling, I moved with the flow of experiences. There was no choice.

The world I would next see was at first mysterious, but became clearer with each passing day. In this world there was something so intrinsically connected to everything that without it our universe

What is is the same with what is not, What is not is the same with what is: Where this state of things fails to obtain, Be sure not to tarry.
—Sêng-ts'an[8]

would not exist. At first it seemed a point from which all things originated. It was a tiny spot—infinitesimal—in my mind, and from this spot I could watch things come into being. As days passed, however, it expanded into the physical world as the very foundation upon which all things rested. I did not perceive this new world as alive, yet it did seem as if everything alive was of it, on it, or connected to it, as planets are suspended in space. Suddenly, my vision grew clearer and *everything* became absolutely *nothing*. I was now in the "world of nothingness."

Any notion of shape or form had disappeared. I was removed, separated from even the memory of the myriad of things existing in life. While I could *see* things in the material world, they were overshadowed to the level of nonexistence by what I saw through them and around them: an enormously pervasive *nothing*. At first I felt bewildered, for I couldn't understand how I could *see* this nothingness. How could *nothing* be seen? And yet I was looking at it! It was all that existed. Nothing.

My body responded to the world of nothingness by feeling lighter—not as if it were floating, but as if my spine were held up by an invisible thread; even my feet seemed to touch the ground more softly. I don't remember exactly how long I remained in the world of nothingness, for there was no mental line drawn from moment to moment. Time seemed to expand and contract, and I often lost track of it. One minute would seem to become an hour and vice versa. In retrospect, I guess I was in this state for less than two weeks.

> *Form is emptiness; emptiness is also form. Emptiness is no other than form; form is no other than emptiness. In the same way, feeling perception, formation and consciousness are emptiness.*
>
> —**Prajnaparamita**[9]

Although time seemed to permute in the world of nothingness, my ordinary sense of time still existed, at least to the degree my everyday life was not hampered. For example, I knew that it would take time to digest my food after a meal, that hours would pass during sleep, and that I would awaken at dawn.

My relationship with the material world also changed while in the world of nothingness. At times, the size of objects eluded my rational observation—something very small could seem enormously large and vice versa. These experiences were not hallucinations. I was simply seeing from a perspective other than usual. We can all use our minds to magnify the infinitesimal and reduce the immense. We can concentrate awareness, focus it, and shoot it with incisive intensity into, for example, a crystalline rock.

One evening I found myself inside of a sparkling geode that had been on my living room table for months. I had been looking into it with a bit of wonderment when suddenly I was swept onto a moving beam of consciousness that took me directly into the geode. Crystals were all I could see. My living room then became the rock itself, and the walls, shimmering amethyst. Looking around, I could see the crystals inside the crystal, then the even tinier particles reflecting light, which warmed me with their energy. I did not intend to take this little trek into the amethyst, but once there I realized I was learning to explore matter from the inside out without fear of losing myself.

There were other unintentional happenings as well. Looking at road maps caused my viewpoint to spontaneously match the perspective from which the map was drawn. In gazing at a map of Chicago, for example, I felt distanced to a place in the atmosphere where I could see the whole city, then I'd need to direct my focus back down to Earth in order to see the map again. Mandalas had a similar effect—my brain patterned itself into the same labyrinthic design, and then, like a mouse in a maze, I had to find my way out of the mandala in order to restore body awareness. Music, however, was enjoyable. I often felt as if I were riding on the notes or hopping from one to the next—bouncing through the soundless on sound itself.

Little by little, I was able to increase my awareness of usual surroundings while having such experiences. Still, the world of nothingness had removed preconceived limitations I had put on the world around me. The mental link to history had been obliterated. My foothold on reality had now become my ability to incorporate new experiences and even enjoy them, if I could. My overriding objective, however, was that I learn from them.

These experiences also reconfirmed something I had learned with the opening of my third eye: that our senses are not limited to our bodies. We can expand our awareness to embrace mountains and constrict it to touch the smallest particle. One could insist all that this is in the mind, but I was seeing that not only is it all *in* the mind, it *is* the mind! As British philosopher and essayist Bertrand Russell once wrote, "The observer, when he seems to be observing a stone, is really, if physics is to be believed, observing the effects of the stone upon himself."[10] In critiquing Russell's statement, which Einstein described as "marvelously concise," Einstein added, "The empirical . . . procedure alone has shown its capacity to be the source of knowledge."[11]

Some scientific thinkers declare that *something* (i.e., this universe) was created from *nothing* (i.e., not anything). Actually, nothing was created from something. Just as the void appeared to be empty (see chapter 1), the nothingness appears to be empty; it's all a matter of appearance. What we need to understand is *function*, not appearances. If something functions, it exists. Actually, the universe was not created out of nothing; it was, and is, created *through* nothing. I will explain.

When the mind is empty of thought, there is nothing to comprehend because *nothing* is there. When a thought arises, the nothingness disappears. It's just that simple. This is not an example of how the world was and is created, it is actual.

The function of the nothing is to serve as the formless space through which all things manifest. It is the blank canvas for creation, the silence between the notes of music, the interval between the heartbeats of the universe; it is the mind free of the constraints of thought. It is that which serves, as Teilhard de Chardin wrote, "to give reality back to us with greater purity."[12]

Meher Baba taught, "Nothing is the shadow of EVERYTHING. . . ." and because this nothing exists, "everything seems to be."[13] This is because the nothing is contained *within* the everything—meaning all of existence as we know it and beyond—so we can distinguish one thing from another in life.

If all things did not have an aspect of nothingness, there would be no myriad of things to discriminate—no space between objects, no movement, not even thought. The universe would be one highly condensed point of energy wherein creation could not exist. Therefore, we need *nothing* in order to have *anything*. And it is *through* nothing—not *from* nothing—that anything can exist, including awareness itself. Nothingness is merely a causeway for energies to manifest as the universe. As such, what has been manifest retains, at least in part—like an invisible genetic code—its inherent characteristic of nothingness. Everything that exists has its own aspect of nothingness.

The world of nothingness is known in Buddhism as the experience of emptiness, or *sunyata*, the Sanskrit term for emptiness. The only objective ground of Truth is that all is nothing. Some students of Zen might consider this to be a rather advanced stage of understanding and experience, but a good teacher would not. To realize that emptiness and form work hand in hand affirms, rather than negates, the universe. An important distinction! Things exist, but they are *transparent*. One sees through the fabric of the manifest world and into the arena where materialization takes place; and this arena is our own *mind*—clear, crisp, sharp, and open to nothingness as reality. In Zen, this is *ku*. According to Zen master Yasutani, *ku* is the "matrix of all phenomena . . . the fundamental principle or doctrine or philosophy of Buddhism."[14]

> *When you have seen true emptiness, emptiness is not empty; complete illumination pervades everywhere.*
>
> —**Chang Po-tuan**[15]

✧   ✧   ✧

The summer of 1973 was approaching and my life, to all appearances, was still going on as usual. I was working hard at the store, traveling, still married to Pete, and enjoying my family and friends. What I've been sharing in this writing happened to me on a mental or spiritual level. Even though there were some physical changes such as rosier cheeks (from fuller breathing) and a smaller belly (a result of improved posture), the only comments from others were that I looked good and seemed more relaxed. Also, somewhere during this time, I grew one-half inch and finally made it to five feet two inches tall, probably from the additional yoga exercises, which can stretch the spine a bit.

All things considered, I guess I was doing OK. Since ego death, I had learned to not take things personally—the good or the bad. I had no defense system set up and ready to go. I didn't need one—there was no one at home to protect. Similarly, there was no one at home to accumulate compliments. Even the most venerable evaluation of another person is not what that person is. To live in Reality, we must realize we are only what God sees us to be. All else is as impermanent as clouds floating in the sky . . .

Now that I had accepted the world of nothingness as an aspect of reality, I could see something corporeal—a *substance* of a sort. It was a sunny Sunday morning. The windows were open, the church bells were ringing, and I was watching the dust fly while cleaning the apartment. I'd always been fascinated with the way little particles floated in the air, but on this day I sud denly became mesmerized with the possibility that there was a dust everywhere, permeating all things—a kind of dust that made all things exist, the stuff that passed through the nothingness to manifest the world as we know it. Barely a moment had passed before I realized this substance was so real I could almost grasp it. The world of nothingness then faded into the background of my consciousness as the natural principle through which the substance materializes itself.

This substance, as I saw it, carried the message that it was the general and nonspecific material from which everything is created, including the pure energy of the universe—even before it has taken form. The substance is the common denominator of the manifest world and exists in a perennial state of manifesting. Once everything is out of the way, the substance is there. When the mind is empty of opposites, complements, and nothingness, it is there.

I knew I was seeing God in this substance, as sure as I knew the face of my best friend. I saw him in everything—everywhere, every waking moment. I was amazed at how our Creator humbled himself so, just for us. He was not too proud to be a glob of chewing gum stuck to the sidewalk, a bag of rotten garbage in a trash can, or even a stream of snot running from a baby's nose. And yet he was not too humble to be resplendent—a tulip, a mountain, or the sun as it warms the earth on a cloudless day. Nor was he too rigid to allow flexibility—a tree swaying with the wind or a wave quietly receding to its source after boldly crashing on the shore. I felt, in placing himself everywhere and in everything, that our Creator graciously gives himself to us. While I knew this substance was only an aspect of him, it was my material connection to him. I sensed I was getting closer to my goal. For the time being, however, I had to be satisfied with communing with God through the omnipresent substance.

This substance showed itself as energy—tangible, corporeal, almost palpable. And yet the solidity of the substance is not the solidity

There can be no creation of something out of nothing. And except for the Absolute Itself there is but nothing. Therefore The Absolute must create the Universe out of Its own "substance.". . .

—Yogi Ramacharaka[16]

we regard in gross matter. Neither is it fluid, like water. There is a particle characteristic to it, but an indistinct one.

We can only pretend human eyes actually see oxygen down to its tiniest particle. Yet this gas is in such a constant state of activity that by the time one little particle is focused upon, it has moved to someplace else and another has taken its place. The amazing thing about this vision is that all particles are the *same* particle! Undifferentiated and generalized, these amorphic particles have no perceptible form—our senses cannot react quickly enough to watch them take form. We would just see the one-particle substance that makes up the gas and know that when it moves, it moves in every direction at the same time—chaotically.

Primordial matter (or *prima materia*, meaning "first matter") is an alchemical term used to describe the essential substance from which all things are made. Alchemy does not begin from the platform of separation of mind and matter. It begins from a perspective in which mind and matter are intrinsic, and God—in creating matter—is *in* it.

> *The Absolute cannot "think" of anything, without putting Itself in that thing, as its Essence.*
>
> —**Yogi Ramacharaka**[17]

The alchemists believed that the mother of all elements (primordial matter) could be found in the material world; moreover, they believed that God himself was in matter, lost and asleep. As Jung wrote in *Psychology and Alchemy*, "For the alchemist, the one primarily in need of redemption is not man, but the deity who is lost and sleeping in matter. . . . His attention is not directed to his own salvation through God's grace, but to the liberation of God from the darkness of matter."[18]

Although alchemists sought God in matter, they also believed there was little difference between matter and mind—a concept embraced within traditions such as Hinduism, Buddhism, and yoga. Because these traditions subject the behavior of matter to the events of the psyche—which is ultimately the Mind of the universe—their approach is more introspective: they seek God, or enlightenment, from within rather than from without.

In Hinduism, *prakriti* is the substance and *purusha* is the influence of the Mind that orders the energy of the substance into form.[19] In yoga, the universe is the Infinite Mind itself, and within that Mind three principles exist: the substance, *chitta*; energy, *prana*; and the product of the two as matter, *akasa*. Yoga also teaches that these principles are actually *one*. They are simply different aspects of God, and those aspects overlap.

In examining faces of God too closely, however, we can lose sight of our purpose for doing so. Wars have been fought and civilizations overturned as we bicker over what's what on this issue. The point is, God is *alive* in this universe—by any name, with any face, and in any tradition. The Creator is not disconnected from one atom of his creation. It is part of the body of his *being*. And if that being is humble enough to lay himself before us, let us walk on his essence during the day and cradle us in his consciousness at night, cannot we refrain from forcing our particular way of seeing God on others? Where is *our* humility? As Saint Thomas Aquinas wrote, "Since the Divine essence is pure act, it will be possible for it to be the form by which the intellect understands. .

. .".[20] This "pure act," when experienced, is humbling beyond words. And when the soul is humbled, there isn't much left but the One who created it, and that One loves his creation as himself.

✣ ✣ ✣

In first seeing this world of substance, I remembered the beatific vision and wondered if its majesty was caused by what I was now seeing: the substance of everything. I was once again in heaven, filled with wonder and secure in my quest. My daily routine remained the same, but I enjoyed it more. I was eager to finish my journey and wanted to see where this substance came from— the Creator, the Godhead. Instead,

For when matter was not yet formed into body . . . it was in disorder. . . .
—Hermes Trismegistus[21]

I was led into the seminal and tumultuous world where the substance resides in pure formlessness, prior to its morphing into the material world. I was suddenly in the "world of possibilities."

Here I could see something similar to what we perceive as space, but not exactly—the activity of the substance is so great there is no real emptiness about this space. Seeing the substance, alive and energized with no sense of order, intelligence, or direction, is seeing Chaos, the *massa confusa* of the alchemists.

The Chinese sage Lao Tzu describes the arena I saw as the "world of possibilities": "There is a thing confusedly formed, born before heaven and earth. Silent and void, it stands alone and does not change, goes round and does not get weary. It is capable of being the mother of the world."[22] The world of possibilities is "confusedly formed" because it has no form and yet it contains the potential for form. It "stands alone and does not change" because of its essential purity. It "goes round" because it moves— it is active—and it "does not get weary" because there is nothing to oppose it. It is "capable of being the mother of the world" because it is pregnant with life. It exists in its original state of purity *in creation* (now) and in an arena *before creation*.

Existing both now and before creation may sound contradictory, but if we are liberated from the linear constraints of time-bound thinking (now, before, after), there is no contradiction. For example, when we look at a distant star, we see it in a particular moment of our time, but what we see may have actually existed millions of years ago, yet those *times* converge with our vision. So it is with the world of possibilities.

But now, O God, tearing open the nether darkness of the universe, you show me that there is another hemisphere at my feet—the very real domain, descending without end, of existences which are, at least, possible.

—Teilhard de Chardin[23]

This world of possibilities is where powerful forces lie in wait to lock energies. I could not see thoughts existent here, only the fundamental energy that predicates the chance of their existence. Because my mind had merged with this world, I was capable of making reality out of something that was not real. I felt as if I'd returned to the Sufi fourth plane, where the powers of creation were at my disposal. Only this time I was not lost in *it*, it was lost in *me*. I was not battling with the powers, I was battling with myself. I didn't know what should or shouldn't be brought into reality; consequently, I had to learn how *not* to let the energies lock together. In other words, I could allow no reality in my mental realm, only its possibility—and the sole way for me to do this was to stop any thought from cohesively forming in my mind.

My teachings from the world of complements (discussed earlier in this chapter) helped me here. I could not let the complements use my energy to precipitate into reality, so I let the half-ideas remain half-ideas by focusing on the "connection of incompleteness," which I had learned was in my mind. And I had to do this while carrying on with normal daily life. I realized, however, that my emotions had to be put on hold while in this world. I knew that the act of *reacting* could make a reality out of a possibility and reacting with *feeling* would give even more concreteness to that newly created reality. I felt that if I let even one possibility become reality, I, like a drop of rain that falls into the ocean, would be absorbed by this world and never make it out. My consciousness would become this vibrating energy and I wouldn't know I ever existed—at least not in the everyday world of light, life, and normality as we commonly know it.

It was here in the world of possibilities that I fully realized the human mind is our servant—our tool. Tricky as it may be at times, the human mind is innocent in its function. We are the ones who blanket the mind's innocence with desire and fear. We call upon these things without realizing it, and the mind, being our servant, responds. We fear and it thinks we *want* to be afraid, we desire and it thinks we *want* to desire. As a result, we wind up with a plethora of whatever we want, filled to the brim with all sorts of fears and desires. And yet the mind is also the tool by which the universe precipitates ideas into the realm of space and time. When the mind finds this out, like an exuberant child taking her first run, it really tries to go to work for us, fulfilling our desires and manifesting our thoughts, *whatever* they may be. If we let this little child run wild in the world of possibilities, it will take us along with it. We might wind up creating something we don't really want; we might wind up believing something is real when it isn't.

After a few days of feeling as if I'd closed my mind to creation, I found a quiet place in this effervescing energy that seemed like the eye of the hurricane. This was not as difficult as it sounds. It was all a matter of not interfering with the forces around me, not doing anything but watching—without fear, without desire. Only then could I remain still enough to maintain mental and emotional balance for normal functioning in the phenomenal world.

Finally able to disassociate from this primordial world of vibrating energies, I could look back and see all the other worlds as orderly dimensions of the world of possibilities. The principles for this order exist at a level beyond the chaotic world of possibilities, while at the same time they underlie it. I understood that those same principles were also in my own mind, as well as in everyone else's mind. Same principles, different vehicles, that's all.

Thus, I had learned that the mind is the universe's instrument for primordial energy to become manifest. This was not a joyful revelation, but it was inescapable. I also knew that everyone else shared this universal responsibility; they just didn't know it. While I trusted that there must have been a good reason for God to have made things this way, I felt as if I needed to tiptoe around my own consciousness in order to not create—

consciously, at least—anything. I was, however, consoled by a sense of underlying direction that everything would come out all right if I stayed out of the way. I could not inject myself into the process.

Although I'd learned that the human mind is essentially involved in creating and perpetuating the universe, everyday life continued. The store was doing well, my marriage was not; but I was now willing and able to face the personal chaos I feared lay ahead.

Pete had lost interest in work and was rarely there. The tales of his machismo continued, only now I believed them. Pete would not listen to my pleas—he wanted no restraints on his behavior. As such, I restrained myself. No longer did I sit and wait for him to come home, worry if he'd been in an accident, or ache as he crawled into bed at dawn, reeking of strange perfume. Because I was in no position to make life-changing decisions, all I could do was continue with my journey and keep my own vows, both spiritual and marital. They provided strength and grounding. Of one thing I was sure: the order I had found behind the world of possibilities was within me.

All the sounds of created being are fused, without being confused. . . .
—**Teilhard de Chardin**[24]

According to Krishnamurti, "The order of nature is order."[25] In other words, since there is nothing outside of nature, there is no such thing as disorder. There is an underlying orderly aspect to chaos with which our minds are unfamiliar. Said another way, there is, in apparent chaos, an order that is imperceptible to us.

In the world of possibilities the mind, exposed to primordial energies on the verge of manifestation, perceives the possibility for anything and everything to occur. As such, the mind sees disorder—without realizing something cannot be put into order if it does not yet exist—and wants to make order out of it. And this is a natural tendency, for our mind is the filter, conduit, and pathway that enables the substance to make its journey from the world of possibilities into the world (thoughts, feelings, objects, and events) as we know it. Carl Jung explains this role in *Psychology and Alchemy*: "The precious substance is potentially contained in this chaos as a *massa confusa* of all the elements rolled into one, and man must diligently apply his mind to it so that 'our heaven' may come into reality. . . ."[26]

What we need to remember, however, is that the moment anything crosses the threshold from the world of possibilities into reality, it *is* in order. "The whole order . . . ," as physicist David Bohm once commented, "includes the order of the universe and the order of the mind."[27] At this very moment, although we may be innocent of it, the substance is finding its way through our consciousness to its proper place in space and time.

While my work schedule continued as usual, I spent less time entertaining myself outside my apartment. My good friend Mary had moved farther away, so I didn't see her except on weekends. Once in a while I'd go to dinner with Aunt Mac or Arta, but that was rare (my store was open late on weeknights and dinner at 9:30 in the evening was a bit late for them). I was spending more and more time alone at home—reading, meditating, and praying. As I look back on this time, I see that the solitary periods were necessary for my growth. There was no other way the integration of the inner and outer worlds could have taken place. Finally I got to a point where I couldn't wait to be alone, for I knew I had the ability to finish my journey if I followed my inner guidance.

As more light was shed upon deeper regions of my consciousness, I was given glimmers of understanding about the threshold between wake and sleep. During nighttime meditation and prayer, I began to notice something unusual occurring before I fell asleep. I would feel myself positioned in the darkness of my mind on one certain spot and knew that if I made one further step, it would be into unconsciousness. For quite a few nights, I was hesitant to take that step—it *felt* like a step—for fear of falling. But after a while I found myself making it into a game, like pausing on the edge of a diving board before leaping off, enjoying the control of the experience. Eventually this became the only way I could go to sleep. I could not go into unconsciousness unless I made the conscious choice to do so. The moment I made the step, it was done.

Passing this threshold between wake and sleep—which I call "conscious crossover"—played an important role in identifying for me where my awareness was cut off. Lingering at the threshold (which is nothing more than deep meditation) allowed me to expand my awareness into the unconscious, thereby bringing its contents to a level where incomplete thoughts and fears could be properly assimilated and redirected into a deeper understanding of myself and the universe. I also understood this threshold to be the very same threshold between sanity and insanity—the "invisible line" I had wondered about when I was working with mental patients: "There seemed an invisible line that, once crossed, temporarily unplugged them from reality" (chapter 1). Now I understood that the line crossed was into the unconscious and that the more conscious we are of the unconsciousness, the more aware we become. The more aware we become, the less power the unconscious has over us, and thus the more power we have over our own existence. This is because we work *with* the powers of creation instead of *against* them.

> *Insanity is possession by an unconscious content that, as such, is not assimilated to consciousness. . . .*
> —Carl Jung[28]

The process of integrating my unconscious into consciousness also presented the opportunity for me to see my past lives. I was under the impression that if my past lives were revealed it would be a little at a time. Amazingly, it all happened at once during meditation one evening. They were all there for me to see. I felt as if someone had given me my life—all of my lives—and presented them right before my eyes: "Here, this is what you have been, if you are curious."

My eyes were closed and I could see a long white marble hallway lined with many doors. I was standing at the end of this glowing, luminous corridor when something told me that behind each door was one of my lives and I was free to open any door. Questions arose: If I opened a door and entered, would I be able to return to the present? Would visiting a past life be similar to sitting in a movie theater as a disconnected spectator? Would I remain untouched by what I would see? Would I *want* to remain? Would I forget where I am in *this* life?

But as I fretted over these questions, I knew I had arrived at a moment culminating all of my past. I decided there was no reason to waste my time on such trifles—especially when I'd just spent so much time and energy trying to clear away so much inner junk! Knowing my past lives didn't seem necessary to my process of enlightenment, and I didn't want to take an "information detour" out of mere curiosity. Thus I declined the invitation to open the doors, at least for the time being . . .

> *As a man casting off worn-out garments takes other new ones, so the dweller of the body casting off worn-out bodies takes others that are new.*
>
> —Bhagavad Gita[29]

As my unconscious continued to open, I entered a new arena, the arena often said to be the realm of psychic experience. I was beginning to find it possible, for example, when talking to a friend to accurately describe places she'd visited and I hadn't. This is sometimes called "mental projection," where people project their minds to another place while consciously remaining in their bodies. To me, however, it felt more like using my mental connection to my friend as a guide, then opening my mind to look and feel.

At first I felt the urge to share my psychic perceptions, but eventually I learned such displays could be frightening to others, especially when I volunteered information. One such day I blurted to a customer, "You just left an apartment of an old building that was freshly painted white. It has a fireplace in the living room with an intricately scrolled mantle. The apartment has no furniture, and you would have rather been riding your horse this day than to have gone there. You are not happy." She glared at me as if I had unearthed some awful secret in her life without permission, then promptly left the store.

She was right. I had been acting like a rude child. What had either of us gained by my invasion into her privacy? Parlor games may be fun, but I shut down the energy that had been focused on my psychic abilities after I decided they were merely games. I didn't know what to do with those abilities and felt that playing with them would delay the completion of my journey. I didn't want to get stuck in psychism, which is nothing more than using the combined senses to perceive subtle energies most of us overlook.

> *Psychism has nothing in it that is spiritual. . . . Psychics merely see on a plane of different material density; the spiritual glimpses sometimes obtained by them come from a plane beyond.*
>
> —H. P. Blavatsky[30]

For a while I traveled a narrow road. Sometimes I felt bombarded with thoughts and feelings I knew were not mine—mental clutter from other people who were either in my proximity or who had recently left the area. Other times I had to figure out if the thoughts or feelings that came upon me *were* mine. During evenings out, it was often necessary for me to leave a restaurant or a room, or avoid being in groups altogether. I had not yet learned how to protect myself from negative thoughts that were entering my consciousness without my consent and draining my energy.

I began to try to visualize an egglike bubble around me, like a force field created by the energy from my psyche. To my amazement, it really worked. There is no trick to it, and it is a handy tool for anyone. It works for two reasons: First, such a psychic field is capable of repelling thoughts that are not on its frequency, much as a plastic raincoat protects one from rain. Second, in order to maintain the egg, one must focus on the physical body, which prevents one from being mentally carried away by negative energies hanging around in the psychic atmosphere. One can still function, talk, and laugh while doing this—and no one else knows.

As I refocused energy past the psychic world, social and familial distinctions faded. Everyone was family. I felt a deep connection with strangers as if they were my next of kin. With no stale distinctions to block my view, my senses seemed to mesh into a network of keener cognition and I experienced the world around me more intensely. It was the same world, but better, brighter, crisper. I could see that each thing had its place and purpose in creation. As if I were glimpsing newly deposited lifeforms spew from beneath the sands of a clear tide pool, I saw nativity in the body of the universe. All of life was closer to me than ever, and I was a part of it. My relationship with the universe was changing, and for the better.

These episodes of understanding, like intermission during a disturbing stage play, provided respite, but with each episode, I wanted for it all to end. I needed rest. But I knew I was not yet back home; still incomplete, blind, and freely riding on the loving forces of creation without giving in return. I did not know how to live.

Physical symptoms continued to occur on the top of my head (seventh chakra), and I began to feel sensations similar to those I'd felt before my third eye opened. According to yoga theory, the crown chakra is the last to open. So I knew my kundalini was on the right track, working with my consciousness to open it. I felt slightly relieved to know there was progress and looked happily forward to the end of my journey.

I had rarely experienced headaches, but they now began to be a daily part of my life, so severe that at times I could barely see beyond the pain. A sledgehammer pounded my brain. I could take no pain relievers because my inner voice forbade it, telling me the headaches would stop when I changed my thinking. Something needed to change, or be adjusted— and I had to find out what it was.

There may be pain, especially in the head, which arises and ceases equally suddenly during the critical phases in the [kundalini] process. The pain . . . [does] not result from the kundalini process itself but from the person's resistance to it.

—Lee Sannella[31]

There were other times when I felt no pain, but my mind felt as if it were split open, and I envisioned blood and fragmented membranes spewing from my head. I could be driving, walking, or talking to someone and suddenly feel my very brain being painlessly torn apart, the way one tears an orange into halves. I could then see the left side of my brain being separated from the right.

I knew no one else could see these visions because they were not happening at the level most people see as reality. But they were as real to me as the breath in my body—which no one else could see either. The last excruciating headache I had was accompanied by the disturbing vision of my brain being split apart and gray matter spewing out. This was the first (and, fortunately, the last) time both the pain and the vision occurred together.

It was a hot summer night. Pete told me he had an appointment with a commodities broker downtown. Because there was no air conditioning at home, I decided to flee the sweltering apartment and ride with him. By this time in our marriage, conversation between us barely took place and it was easy for me to turn inward without notice. I was determined and upset at the same time—determined to find out what was causing my headaches and messy visions, and upset with the disintegration of my marriage.

As it turned out, Pete's meeting place was a bar on Clark Street. I didn't want to join him inside, so I waited in the car and tried to meditate away my headache while remaining open to why I was in pain to begin with. In looking back, I have absolutely no recollection of what happened the rest of that evening. All I remember is a blinding headache, sweltering heat, and a struggle for peace.

The next day I felt better, but then I began to see something strange. While standing at the kitchen sink with my hands propped on the cold ceramic, I was taking a moment of silence after washing my lunch dishes. For no apparent reason, the vision of a flower came to me. At first I thought my imagination had conjured up this vision to counterbalance the headaches I'd recently been having. Then it became clear that something was growing on top of my brain. It was a flower—larger and more beautiful than any I'd ever seen—extending from my brain beyond the boundaries of my body.

Initially my vision of this flower was vague, as if I were seeing it through a vast and foggy darkness. Moving closer with my inner sight, I saw clearly what looked like a combination of an upside-down rose and a water lily. Bathed in moonlight, it reflected the deep hues of a forest at night, where specks of light and shadow move with the breeze. Then, when I tried to discern the petals, I found myself underneath one. Either the flower had grown to enormous proportions or I had shrunk—I didn't know which. All I could see was one huge petal, hovering over me. Then I saw this petal gently rising, and I felt as if I were helping it open. My arms pushed it upward as my feet merged with the earth, my energy drawn from my refusal to succumb to my fear of what was underneath the petal: the unknown.

The opening of the first petal gave me understanding as to the cause of my exploding headaches and grisly visions: I had been trying to stop the flower from opening. In wanting my integration process to end, in wanting to quit learning about the unconscious mind and its connection to the creative powers of the universe, I was resisting an imperative. This flower *had* to open.

At the time, I made no conscious connection between this flower and my readings of Hindu yoga theory. When one is so deeply embedded in the unconscious mind, consciously connecting one thing to another is as difficult as trying to understand the meaning of a dream while still in the dream. Focus becomes intense, even to the exclusion of memory. So this flower was just there, and I saw it, felt it.

I no longer doubted my sanity. Finally, the true knowledge of inner transformation overrode all doubt. I did not know what would happen next, what the opening of the next flower petal would reveal, but I did know that to stop the opening of the flower would be detrimental to my psyche and my body. Movement and unfoldment are change, which evokes resistance. Resistance causes suffering. Accepting pain diminishes resistance. No resistance, no pain.

With the passage of days, I began to feel and see each petal as it started to open. Initially, each began with a fear I'd projected into my life. It did not matter what the fear may have been about, when it had come upon me, or if it even made sense—and most of the time it didn't. What mattered was that the whole concept of fear needed to be dissolved, yet I could not identify exactly what I was afraid of. And that's the tricky part: the mind wants to make the unknown a known, so it thinks of things *to* fear. I quickly discovered it was not the object of my fear that needed to be dissolved or worked through, for that was only a projection from my mind—that was dutifully but ineffectually endeavoring to identify a reason for my fearfulness—sheer displacement. With this understanding, I realized all my fears were one: I was afraid only of the unknown.

All other fears I then pushed aside as impertinent. If one caught me in its clutches, I'd look for a petal and try to understand whatever it wanted to teach me. Sometimes it was a struggle—like untying knots in my brain—to receive understanding; other times, by simply remaining open to the unknown, I would suddenly gain a completely new perspective on something with no effort at all. The funny thing about this process, I realized, was that the smallest things seemed to teach the biggest lessons.

One lesson in particular came from a toddler. I had already

unraveled the human complex of guilt and the process of judgment, at least to my comfort level. I had seen forgiveness and nonaction and experienced the levels of creation, but I felt I'd missed something along the way, and it was nagging at me like a toothache. Then, one day while working at the store, a customer came in the door with a baby in her arms. He was barely a year old, still drooling, sticky faced and sticky fingered with a red sucker, I was sure, stuck somewhere to his clothes. I only hoped the mom would not let him run loose.

No sooner did that thought enter my mind than she put him down. Gasping as he gleefully stumbled toward a rack of silk blouses, I swooped him up and dangled my keys in hopes he would stay quiet. When he began to stare at me as if I were the silly one, I looked into his clear blue eyes and suddenly envisioned the things he would accomplish in life and the mistakes he would make, the selflessness he would exhibit and the transgressions he would commit. I felt God loved this child unfathomably and that no matter what kind of person he grew to be in his life, God would always love him as he loved him that moment. God would never judge him or chide him, push him aside or discount him in any way. He would always and forever be there the instant this child called. This child was his son!

As he was carried out of my store, this child was perfect in every way—drool, sticky red face and hands, and all. I knew I would never again look at children as underdeveloped creatures that should not be allowed out of the home until trained. That was what I had been missing: a love for children. And as I turned inward on this, I realized the helplessness that I had felt as a child because of my mother's illness. I also realized I still had steps to retrace in my journey, as well as much more to learn in the process of going forward.

Most of us have seen paintings or sculptures of a flower that resembles a large lotus blossom, on which saints or bodhisattvas sit in peaceful repose. Other depictions place the flower above the heads or

The thousand-petalled lotus flower opens. . . . Because of the crystallization of the spirit, a hundred-fold splendour shines forth.
—**The Secret of the Golden Flower**[32]

surrounding the entire bodies of enlightened ones. Because it stems from ancient Hindu yoga theory, many would think this flower is a philosophic metaphor, but it is not. This flower is real and it can be seen—literally—by one who experiences the opening of the crown chakra at the top of the head. This chakra is also called *sahasrara*, meaning "thousand." Here is the home of the flower of a thousand petals.

Eastern art scholar Ajit Mookerjee describes the spiritual significance of the lotus flower: "The inverted lotus . . . *Sahasrara* is the centre of quintessential consciousness, where integration of all polarities is experienced, and the paradoxical act of transcendence is accomplished in passing beyond ever-changing *samsara* [life with birth and death], and 'emerging from time and space.'"[33]

Kundalini—in conjunction with consciousness—opens the petals of this flower. Kundalini is a connective energy that exists within all of us, and the extent to which the kundalini has been activated and channeled corresponds directly to one's spiritual understanding or development. Within each petal is a lesson, and each petal that opens includes past lessons—as if somehow our steps are retraced in order to go forward. (Examples of this are written earlier in this chapter: I used what I had learned about half-ideas in the world of complements in order to surpass the world of possibilities. I learned from a toddler how to face my own childhood helplessness, share in God's love for all children, appreciate their courage, and be humbled at their innocence.)

As such, understanding is not always complete on the first go-around. There are, as I experienced, often some things left behind to remind us of our own human nature, our individual likes and dislikes, our personality. We can "clean our house" as much as we want, but there is still the person cleaning it, and that is the part of us that won't wash away; that is the part of ourselves that—one way or another—we need to accept.

Meanwhile, let's not forget that "kundalini" is only a word to describe an energy that enables us to better understand our existence in this universe, our Creator, and, ultimately, Truth. As I stated earlier, kundalini is energy that *becomes* understanding—but this will not happen without our being conscious of it. Yet the power of kundalini should not be underestimated. Like a strict teacher, it sometimes inflicts pain, other times joy, but it never gives plaudits. Pride is not allowed. We all live with the kundalini and feel its effects because we are subject to the power of kundalini at all stages of our development. As contemporary teacher and healer Rosalyn L. Bruyere tells us, "The kundalini is our primary means of sensing life and physical reality. Our secondary means is the nervous system, which transmits the energy of the experience or event first recorded by and in the kundalini to the brain via the spinal cord."[34]

When the last three chakras are opened—throat, forehead, and crown—we have greater awareness of the workings of the unconscious mind. Once the seventh chakra is activated, we begin to have awareness of union with all creation. Perhaps we will even see the flower, the lotus of love for all beings.

The flower is not seen the way we would normally visualize something. Because it is viewed as residing both inside and outside the body, the perception is twofold. Inner vision is accompanied by outer vision, as if one is standing simultaneously within and without the flower. Perhaps the dual perspective is because its connection to our being is not merely psychic. As Dr. Rammurti S. Mishra states, the chakra where the flower resides is "located in the cerebral cortex."[36]

Look for the flower to bloom in the silence that follows the storm. . . . Not until the whole nature has yielded and become subject to its higher self, can the bloom open.
—Light on the Path[35]

The flower is both personal and transpersonal. It is part of all of us, and yet each one of us must deal with its lessons on a personal level. To put it another way, after one sees the flower, one may contend that people do not garden flowers. Rather, flowers garden people. Or, as Alan Watts once remarked, "You did not come into this world, you came out of it."[37]

We all know that we are here as a result of the reproduction process. We also know that the biological aspect of our being is not all there is to us. In an effort to understand the real why and wherefore of things, we look to religion, philosophy, or some form of divination to make sense out of the world for us. In our search for truth, we also turn to science; it provides an almost palpable structure that reason cannot defy.

The distinction between science and mysticism is not as broad as some people believe. Where science seeks proof, mysticism has realization. In science, questions usually precede answers, but when a scientist gets an answer to a question, that answer *is* a realization. In mysticism, answers usually precede questions—for in mystical experiences, one often finds answers to questions never asked. Intellectual desire for expansion is, in essence, the same as spiritual desire for wholeness.

> *It finally turns out that one can, after all, not get along without "metaphysics." The only thing to which I take exception there is the bad intellectual conscience which shines through between the lines.*
>
> **—Albert Einstein**[38]

Ultimately, I found myself wondering what the questions were—especially regarding my experiences of the "worlds." In my dilettantish understanding of physical theory, I concluded that the mystic sees how the universe works, while the scientist works to see the universe. Yet between the two, there is little or no disparity. In looking for the unseen, delving into the unknown, they both serve to enrich our existence.

My intrigue with quantum cosmology led me to see the worlds in the theories of our great physicists/mathematicians. I could see the world of opposites in Paul Dirac's "antimatter,"[39] the world of complements and the connection of incompleteness in Werner Heisenberg's "uncertainty principle,"[40] the world of nothingness in a singularity (a point of space-time where the known laws of physics do not apply, predicted by Einstein's general theory of relativity and corroborated by the work of Roger Penrose and Steven Hawking), the world of substance in John Bell's theorem of nonlocality,[41] and the world of possibilities in David Bohm's multidimensional "quantum potential."[42]

Each day science learns more about the universe, so who knows what new corollaries we can make tomorrow? We now have invisible matter ranging from the size of tiny particles with infinitesimal mass to the size of planets ("neutrinos" and "machos"), strings and superstrings (whose vibrations orchestrate manifestation), and "space-time foam," which predicts that loop quantum gravity composes physical space—meaning basically that space is not empty. But philosophers, alchemists, and mystics have known this for centuries.

The mystical world of the ancients is now the modern world of science. As brilliant, exciting, and potentially productive as new discoveries may be, they reveal complexities of the universe that the ancients pointed to centuries ago. We learn, and the more we learn, the more we want to know, and so on. And this is fun! But it never fails to amaze me that knowledge of the principles by which this universe was and is created has no bearing on the principles

> *Quantum mechanics is certainly imposing. But an inner voice tells me that it is not yet the real thing. The theory says a lot, but does not really bring us any closer to the secret of the "Old One." I, at any rate, am convinced that He is not playing dice.*
> —Albert Einstein[43]

themselves. In other words, identifying the molecular structure of water does not change the nature of water or its purpose in the universal scheme of things—we still need to drink it.

We all have the ability to anticipate experiences as well as the ability to remember them. The "anticipation" is what we think of as future; the "remembering" is what we think of as past. If we had no memory, we would have no anticipation. Anticipation of our future is based upon what we have experienced at some point in our past, even if it was just a fleeting thought. We also sense there are hidden forces over which we have no control working in our lives. Whether it's a cancelled flight, a bout with the flu, or a flat tire, we don't actually know from moment to moment what will happen to us, to those we love, or to the entire existence of humankind for that matter. So we find a comfort level in probability—what predicates a likely event—and we find a pattern to work with. In other words, I know that if I do "this," "that" will most likely happen.

But no one can predict with certainty what will happen because we cannot see the entire pattern of existence. Why can't we? Because we are a part of the pattern. Similar to our capacity to remember and anticipate, this pattern combines the past and the future into the present of here and now; thus it is always changing. This pattern—also known as "karma"—is the order behind the chaos I saw in my journey. Every event we experience is first drawn from the world of possibilities, concentrated into probabilities, then precipitated through the pattern as an event.

Like us, God plays dice—He, too, knows only the odds.

—**Physicist Heinz R. Pagels**[44]

Some believe karma is purely a law of cause and effect. Others believe it is some kind of report card to God for good deeds, bad deeds, and the remuneration of both. While these ideas may be partially true, I see them as limiting and narcissistic dogma. Karma is more than those things. It is the mechanism through which the universe may operate without conflict by orchestrating all action in space-time while promulgating the underlying order behind the world of possibilities. I also understand karma to be the ethereal barrier between action and nonaction, the partition between the two spheres of time and eternity that I saw on the evening I experienced the Tao (chapter 4).

The dynamic karma uses to support the creative principles of order is *accommodation;* the action it incorporates is *balance*; the system it creates is a *pattern*. Karma designs the pattern for action in the universe, which changes the moment anything happens, so it is a continual state of flux. Lastly, karma cannot change anything, but it is the gatekeeper for personal change—which can change everything.

In my earlier interpretation of Dogen's concept of being time, we saw that our own individuality has a personal time, which is contained within the context of universal time, or eternity. We are each our own quantum field within the laws of karma. Yet, insignificant as it may seem, we change our pattern with every thought, every observation, and every action. We are cocreators of the world we see around us.

The uncertainty and incompleteness we feel deep within our being is life *before* manifestation and life *as* it is manifest. This uncertainty is *tanha*, the thirst for becoming—the continual exchange of complementary energies of the perceived opposites

*Is God making this up
as She goes along?*
    —Physicist Leon
        Lederman[45]

of being and nonbeing. This uncertainty and incompleteness is the past becoming the future in the eternity of the present—karma—the beautiful and ever-changing pattern of life that accommodates and balances all things in the universe so they may interact without conflict.

We, too, are a part of this becoming. We want power, yet we do not want the uncertainty that comes with it. We want certainty but realize it is only illusion. So where is the end to it all? And do we even *want* an end?

As to what was happening to me in that summer of 1973, I had learned that *this* moment is as complete as things get and that *this* world is the culmination of all the worlds I had seen in my journey. Yet I knew there were more lessons to come, more petals to open in the flower. What I did not know was that it would all happen at once. In one moment of magnificence I would reach my goal.

Chapter 6

THE GOAL

Much ado about everything . . .

I T WAS NOW JULY. ALTHOUGH I WANTED TO BE CLOSER TO GOD, I really didn't want to *know* more. I was tired of having entire new worlds unfold before me, tired of wondering if I would be able to handle the next revelation, tired of learning about the metaphysical aspects of life. Since everything had turned out OK so far—the world was still the world and I was still in it—I'd managed to keep my sanity and was functioning well. The best thing for me to do now was to begin paying more attention again to what was going on around me.

That summer of 1973 we still had a "hippies versus red-necks" situation across the country, where the length of some-one's hair or style of dress was judged as an ostensible display of ideals. Since all types shopped at the store, I would wear a business suit one day and jeans with a funky blouse the next. I even wore a headband with a peace symbol once or twice, until a customer politely told me I was wearing it upside down.

Although I wondered about the country's political issues, for the most part I stayed out of the debate. I felt nothing could ever be changed until we first became content with our own discontent and worked from inside our deepest self to help others. To me, a radical point of view was (and is) a part of the world of opposites, which brings about an undesired result along with the desired. Lastly, I saw political discontent, marital discontent, or discontent in general as symptom of something much more insidious than the issues most often identified as the causes. When we try to change circumstances without looking at what may need changing within ourselves, the fundamental causes for our frustration will remain hidden. Self-avoidance is self-betrayal.

The past few months had been filled with incredible experiences that I now saw as pieces of a living puzzle, each part having its own place and purpose in the matrix of existence. God had shared the secrets of the universe with me, given my eyes and heart the vision to see the world's magnificence, and shown me love beyond comprehension. I was within him and he within me; I was surrounded and enraptured. I lived for the day when I could embrace our Creator totally.

> *I am consoled to hear the clock strike, for in the passing away of that hour it seems to me that I am drawing a little closer to the vision of God.*
>
> —Saint Teresa of Avila[1]

I felt my trials were nearly over and I sensed everlasting peace almost within my reach. I believed I could surmount the obstacles remaining between me and God without much of a problem, with one exception: I had a fear of a heavy darkness that seemed like an enormous storm cloud hovering ominously in my mind. I did not understand this cloud, but it felt like pure, powerful potential, ready to destroy all that came in its path. And it was looming closer with each passing day. I soon realized I would have to face this darkness, which was not the darkness of the void, not the darkness of the devil, not the darkness of the unknown. This darkness, unbeknownst to me, would be the dark side of God himself . . .

Barely a week had passed since I had seen the *sahasrara* flower in my brain. Although I was afraid of the dark cloud that was upon me, I had learned the paradoxical aspect of fear: that the more we run from it, the closer the object of our fear becomes—that *not* wanting something is actually calling it into play, as the world of opposites teaches. So I thought perhaps the cloud could be successfully managed by not fighting, not resisting its power—which I perceived could demolish me. While I didn't see a reason for the doom I was facing, I trusted that God would not have taken me this far in my journey only to have my consciousness destroyed. I believed my teachings would hold me steadfast and that with God's help I would withstand the assault.

Yet as I fought by *not* fighting, the cloud grew darker, heavier, and more foreboding, as if it carried within itself nothing but death. Then, like an unrelenting steamroller, it began to flatten my consciousness—everything I'd ever known or felt was being slowly squished into one unending plane of misery in which I could not think or imagine and beyond which I could not move. I felt as if I were being buried alive. Help! My safe haven had been God, my heavenly Father who had been with me every step of the way in the journey. I called for him.

He was the one who had shed light into the void, then protected me from negative forces; the one who had broken the chains of my intellect, then revealed the powers of thought itself; the one who had given me life after death, then filled me with love for all things. He had *always* been there to lead me out of confusion. Time and time again he had soothed my soul with his love and strength. I was now calling him once more, but as this cloud became more oppressive, God became more distant and more difficult to find.

I began to feel a crushing weight from this cloud, so severe it seemed it would squash me completely. At the same time, I felt all of humankind was in the same danger, even if they didn't know it. There was no outside to my mind—everything was *inside* it, where the forces of creation were being subverted by the forces of destruction. I felt compelled to support the manifest world with my own consciousness or it would compress, then explode into nothingness.

The darkness intensified. My mental vision gradually dimmed until I was blind—not physically blind, for I could see objects in the everyday world, but blind in my *mind*. This blackness was pressing on me and obstructing my inner vision, cognition, and communication with my God. I had lost him.

God was gone and my broken heart could not understand how this could be happening. I wished every cell in my body would devour itself while the cries of my soul echoed into oblivion. My God had deserted me and I realized that this time I was truly dead! The cloud had taken him from me. But how could anything be more powerful than my Father? *Where, for God's sake, was he?*

The days that followed are almost a blur. I remember a weekend trip to Springfield for the wedding of my dear friend Pam. The elegant reception was held in the ballroom of a restored Gothic home, but during this celebration I was merely a walking corpse without a soul, a zombie. Unlike Atlas, the weight of the world wasn't on my shoulders, it was in my head. It seemed like when I moved, all of creation moved with me—and if I moved too quickly, everything would quake apart. I was trying to survive this oppression, support the universe, and contain the cloud all at the same time. I feared that at any moment my brain would burst. And the more I feared, the less control I had of the cloud. When I could no longer contain it, I saw its malignant fog seep from the egresses of my mind, slowly shroud the room, then mercilessly consume even the last suggestion of life. Bleak, heavy, dead—all was devoured.

I climbed the winding staircase, as if to distance myself from what I had just seen. The sun beamed through beveled windows, yet I could feel no warmth. The room was filled with people, yet I could hear little sound. Life had disappeared. Everything and everyone was, and always had been, dead. We all existed in a place before life was conceived, and from that place we remained unborn.

Sitting quietly, I watched everyone and wondered if they knew of the deadness. Was their pretense about life conscious, or was it blindly spontaneous? Yet as I watched the joy of the wedding party, the sharing, the companionship, it occurred to me they did not really know about the powerful darkness. They were innocent of it all—and in their innocence, life operated *through* them. In other words, it was precisely through their ignorance of the darkness that they existed.

On the one hand, I did not know quite what to do about this discovery; on the other hand, I felt it really didn't matter what I did. Above all, however, I could not speak of it. I knew life existed for others only because they *believed* the illusion. I also knew that the only light in the world came from their very eyes.

Words cannot adequately describe the extent to which the cloud overpowered, crushed, then sucked all things in life into its heavy darkness. There was an astounding difference between experiencing ego death (see chapter 2) and enduring the dark cloud. With ego death I had lost the image of myself, but I had lost merely an illusion. In its place my life had become filled with the love of God and love for the universe. Now, however, I had been abandoned in a world that never was, my being reduced to infinite deadness, bereft of even the memory of life. All of creation had been condensed into one plane of lifeless potential and I was frozen in the middle of it; my mental eye could see nothing.

Upon returning to my hotel room I wondered what force, what purpose, what desire, what entity had caused this illusion of life for humankind—of humankind. There had to be something behind it all. Yet as I wondered, I realized all I could do was wait.

The soul feels itself to be perishing . . . in a cruel and spiritual death . . . devoured in the darkness. . . .

—Saint John of the Cross[2]

While waiting, I realized what foolishness is. In the absolute sense, it is indifference to God's omnipotence. I had believed not only *in* God, but I'd understood him to be all there is, including the self of every person. I had loved him, but in the end, I saw it was not really God that I had been loving—for until he was gone, I'd had no idea, no conception of his *greatness.*

I did not know I could have any new perceptions about God, especially when I could not see him, but I did. In this time of unsurpassed loneliness, my heart opened up to see what was *not* there, and by seeing what was *not* there, I knew what had been there. And I felt bereft without it.

Somewhere within this bleak contemplation, I began to see myself as beyond repair. I could not change my nature and would continue to blindly devour life as if it were a right and not a gift, as if nothing mattered but attainment, goal seeking, and satisfaction. I'd been given knowledge and couldn't use it, been shown glory and walked away from it, been enraptured and still sought more to stockpile in my own little piece of eternity. I'd wanted to pierce the heavens and claim God for my own. Yes, I'd been devouring life, just like the dark cloud that had overtaken my mind. Yet I saw no other way for me to exist. So this was the end. I could go no further. I had found my beastly nature—my human nature. I was sure that no new realization could stop me from walking on God's universe in complete recklessness, destroying all in my path with my appalling, contemptible, and all-too-human nature.

With these thoughts I became aware I was, once again, in a state of repentance. Although I wanted so desperately to be near God, I felt

> *How lenient the punishment in hell was in comparison with the place I deserved.*
>
> —Saint Teresa of Avila[3]

I was completely undeserving of him, his absolute perfection, his glorious love. While it seemed almost unendurable to forfeit the greatest love in my life, I decided *not* to have God near and resolved to stick with it. Done. Finished!

This martyrdom lasted throughout the night. The next morning I came to see this self-placating mitigation as artificial, a slice of sanctimonious baloney, an easy way out. In taking a deeper look at myself, I saw that what I *really* wanted was nothing more than sheer and utter *control*. And to gain control, I was pushing God out of the way, rejecting him. When I understood this self-deception, I also understood that in the act of rejecting God, I was also rejecting myself, for God was the only *real* part of me.

Exposed! Caught in my own game of self-deception, I suddenly realized that *anything* I did would still be playing the game. If I were to find one place to hide, one desire to be fulfilled, one fear to run from—even one thing to sacrifice—I would still be playing the game. And this was a game I was tired of. This was a game that was not real. This was a game I could not win. I surrendered.

In *this* surrender there was no abyss into which to plunge myself. There was nothing left to even think about. I didn't know what I was surrendering *to*—I *could* not know. Questioning anything would have brought me back into the game. One might suppose the feeling of surrendering to something unknown might be mysterious, but I wasn't mystified. I couldn't think beyond the dimension to which my consciousness had been flattened—a dimension of no life, light, or escape.

With surrender comes an awareness of how difficult life becomes by our self-created mountains of resistance. We gnaw at our skins and then wonder why there

> *Only when he learns to cease thinking of himself at all, in however depreciatory a sense; when he abolishes even such a selfhood as lies in a desire for the sensible presence of God, will that harmony be attained. This is . . . the utter surrender. . . .*
>
> —Evelyn Underhill[4]

are sores all over our bodies. We then go back and nibble at the sores in hopes of eliminating them. But when we chew at the sores of our souls, we are attempting, without knowing it, to engulf the unconscious with the conscious mind. Struggling to cram the infinite into the finite is as futile as trying to swallow an ocean instead of learning to swim—all in an effort to get our feet on dry land. With complete surrender, however, the dry ground of usual consciousness no longer exists. It has been transformed to accommodate something much more encompassing. It has found its home in the Unconscious.

> *Consciousness so called may thus be regarded as the field where the Unconscious functions.*
> —D. T. Suzuki[5]

I was in this state of surrender the day after the wedding, scarcely able to navigate the obligatory farewells before heading back to Chicago. Days came and went before I was able to again perceive life. On the third (or, perhaps, fourth) morning, a thought came that awakened me: I thought of my *self*. That moment, I realized I had been in a comalike state, with no self-awareness, for days. During those dark days I had slept, eaten, and worked as usual. I had continued my life, but I didn't remember doing so. When my cognitive abilities returned, I assumed I had somehow acted normally during those days, as no one had indicated otherwise.

Thankfully, I was again able to see life around me and in me. Not all at once, but more like a slow rising of consciousness from the depths of hell (where there was no God or self) to a place where life exists. That's just how it happened. The darkness was

But after three and a half days a breath of life from God entered them, and they stood up on their feet. . . .
—**Revelation 11:11**

no more. Life and consciousness were again a part of my being.

When my sense of being alive returned, I prayed to accept *everything* as a part of my existence, even suffering. Why? I do not know, except to say I felt I could not return to life without accepting the predicament in which human beings find themselves. I was one of them. If life were again to become a reality, I had to accept it entirely—the agony and the ecstasy.

My flippant disconcern regarding the cloud, or how it had changed me, was balanced by a foreboding that I would one day find out. For now, I was just happy to feel alive again. No longer was I anathematized in a flat plane of deadness. I had regained inner vision—could see my own thoughts and actions in relation to the world around me—and things were returning to normal.

When I had seen the dark cloud overtake all things, I was seeing the potential that predicates life itself—the energy that

Enlightenment is the illuminating of this dark region, when the whole thing is seen at one glance, and all intellectual inquiries find here their rationale.
—**D. T. Suzuki**[6]

exists/existed before even the idea of life was conceived. What I had perceived as dead was simply not yet born, not yet a reality, not yet in a state of *being*. Like suffocating in the darkness of my mother's womb, suffering the dark cloud was my experience of being *unborn*. It was also enduring, as I sometimes call it, the dark side of God.

Here is what I have come to understand about that aspect of God: God existed before creation of the universe as we know it. Prior to creation, God was not *conscious* of creation. How could he be? Nothing was made yet. And because God still *is*, that part of him that is *unconscious* to creation still *is*. This same unconscious state is none other than *our* very own unconscious mind. Being conscious in the depths of the universal Unconsciousness is the experience of the dark cloud. Life itself is yet to begin; unfathomable potential is all that exists.

The term *cosmic Unconsciousness* was used by D. T. Suzuki to denote the creative power of the universe in a latent state, "God even prior to his creation." Suzuki explains: "Psychologically speaking, satori is super-consciousness, or consciousness of the Unconscious. The Unconscious is not, however, to be identified with the one psychologically postulated. The Unconscious of satori is with God even prior to his creation. It is what lies at the basis of reality, it is the cosmic Unconscious."[7]

The cosmic Unconscious is quite different from cosmic consciousness or the personal unconscious. It underlies and supersedes both. Hui nêng (638 713), the sixth patriarch of China, wrote, "He who understands the teaching of the Unconscious has a most thoroughgoing knowledge of all things. He who understands the teaching of the Unconscious sees into the spiritual realm of all Buddhahood. He who understands the 'abrupt' teaching of the Unconscious reaches the stage of Buddhahood."[8] What I believe Hui-nêng is saying is that understanding the teachings of the Unconscious is illumination. Understanding the teachings *abruptly*—all at once, in one moment—is enlightenment.

Experiencing the dark cloud also led me to understand what is known in Zen as the "Unborn." Japanese Zen master Bankei (1622–1693) used this concept in his teachings, and it boils down to this: We are never really born, we only think we are. The concept of being born or of dying is moot when we are conscious beyond the illusion of *samsara* (birth and death). This consciousness is the "unborn" and eternal source of *being*. In one of his sermons Bankei preached, "The Unborn that I am talking about is the Buddha mind. The Buddha mind is unborn, and it illuminates the mind. In the Unborn everything is properly ordered. Those who carry out all things according to the Unborn find their eyes open to other persons so that they today can behold all other living persons as Buddhas."[9]

Bankei also negates the concepts of *achieving* enlightenment, Buddhahood, or salvation. He taught that we already have it: "When you're awake, you're awake in the same Buddha-mind you were sleeping in. You sleep in the Buddha-mind while you sleep and are up and about in the Buddha-mind while you're up and about. . . . You're never apart from it for an instant. . . . There's not a moment when you're not a Buddha."[10] (What a joyous sense of release Bankei imparted to those living under samurai rule! To this day, he is loved and admired by many in Japan.)

Consciousness is an instrument of experience for the Unconscious. Whether we are awake or asleep does not matter, for the world we experience as the dream world or material world is nothing more than our own mind. *Both* are the Unconscious— and the Unconscious is One Mind. Since this One Mind cannot be objectified, there is *no mind*. It is unborn.

The Buddhist teachings of no mind (*wu-shin*), the doctrine

of the Unconscious (*wu-nien*), and the Unborn (*fushō*) are misinterpreted when instead of dispelling illusion they negate reality. The point of these teachings is to lead us beyond our usual sense of life and death, joy and pain, love and anger, and into a living consciousness that is eternal, all knowing, and at peace with all things. This consciousness is of the Unconscious.

> *The Unconscious is the true Mind, the true Mind is the Unconscious.*
>
> —Bodhidharma[12]

"Satori," as Suzuki wrote, "makes the Unconscious articulate."[11]

Initially, being awake in the cosmic Unconscious is terrifying. For me, it seemed a dark cloud had overtaken all things, including my heavenly Father. According to Meher Baba, "This is the only state where 'God Is Not' and 'Consciousness Is.'"[13] As I see it, this is because everything is removed from consciousness *but* God. There is nothing for consciousness to be separate from; consciousness *is* God. But we, as human beings, cannot know this during the experience of the cloud because we are *completely* absorbed by him—blinded by the great potential—and there is no room for even an inkling of objectification. As Baba goes on to say, "The reality, however, is that God Is," and he continues with a similar conclusion: "As it can never happen for God not to exist . . . God [in this state] plays the part of consciousness itself, which consciousness is sometimes termed super-consciousness. . . ."[14]

In this state, I felt as if I were in a coma—not physically, but mentally. Because the outside world had been engulfed by the Unconscious, my focus was not on remaining conscious in the outside world, it was on remaining conscious in the Unconscious.

If I could not remain conscious there, I would not remain conscious at all.

During my three or four dark days, where (in retrospect) I was essentially sleepwalking, I was in the state that Sufi mystics refer to as "nirvana." In Sufism, nirvana is not synonymous with heaven, nor does it refer to the Buddhist nirvana of release. (Literally translated from Sanskrit, *nirvana* means "blowing out, or extinguishing.")[15] To Sufi mystics, nirvana means "vacuum"—"the very same vacuum state as the original state of God,"[16] according to Meher Baba, the "state of God in original, divine sound sleep."[17] The only difference between this sleep state of God and *our* sound sleep state is in our awareness of it—our being conscious in the Unconscious.

> *When one goes into divine sleep one must wake up in the Divine.*
> —**Meher Baba**[18]

Experiencing the dark cloud is also the biblical "second death": "Blessed and holy is he who shares in the first resurrection! Over such the second death has no power. . . ." (Revelation 20:6). Although many of the symbols represented in Revelation may be meaningful only to its author, as with most alchemical texts, the underlying message is a universal theme in which we all share.

Surviving ego death is (to use biblical phraseology) the *first* resurrection. We are then prepared to go forward and see through illusion, master the will, face demons in the collective unconscious, traverse the levels of creation, endure the dark cloud, and, at last, surrender.

It was now mid-July. I was relishing life after surrender and didn't think much about the dark cloud or what it may have done to me while I was engulfed by it. God had returned to my life and I was alive again, as was everyone else. Whew!

I'd completed a short buying trip to Los Angeles and was again back home in Chicago. Work and play, wakefulness and sleep—all seemed to meld into one effortless stream of bliss. Without a worry in the world, I was functioning better than ever.

The chakra on top of my head had begun to feel more activity than it had in the past few months. Feeling sensations at this chakra when I was meditating was not unusual, but now the sensations were intensifying, as they had done prior to the opening of my third eye. They were also occurring when I wasn't meditating. At times, it felt as if the blunt end of a broomstick was pressing down on the top of my head. Other times, it felt as if that same spot was having minor spasms.

I was not concerned about these sensations because I'd learned from yoga theory that the opening of this chakra portends complete enlightenment. It is the "boss" of all chakras, so to speak. I was looking forward to the end of my journey. (I should say here that experts on chakra theory agree that chakras are "activated" or "energized" by the kundalini, but some refrain from using the word *opened*. I use the word *opening* because that's what it *feels* like when chakras are activated—especially the chakras located in the forehead and the top of the head.)

I began to live in a state of "meditation in action" (see chapter 2) almost constantly. In the past I had enjoyed working at the store, but I'd often procrastinated about doing household chores— I'd found them boring. But now, doing laundry and washing windows was a joy for me because I could marvel at God while doing those things. He kept me company and showed me a deep understanding of the workings of the universe. The prosaic had become profound. I was again experiencing the beautific vision, only this time God was not just in the vision, he was also within me. Yet somehow he remained God, alive in this perfectly ordered universe. My thanks to him for creating consistency and order in the phenomenal world grew with each passing day. Soon, everything I did became a devotion. I had to give everything to him, because everything *was* his.

Prayer filled my head as continuously as breath filled my lungs. The name of God rang in my mind, incessant as my heartbeat, and I did not know why. It almost seemed there was a recorded tape playing the song of my soul, the words of which consisted only of praises to God, my Father, my Love, my Lord. I could think of nothing else to call him, so these names were silently repeated over and over, day and night, until they became the predicate to every thought, every movement. But I also knew the names did not matter, for there are many names from many religions in many different languages. It is not the appellation that matters. If we had never heard the word *God* at all, our souls would find a way to adore him. In fact, that is what humankind *has* done, although we tend to get lost in the words we have conjured up and the ceremonies we have devised, taking them for truth instead of the symbols they are.

> *So for the sake of your tradition, you have made void the word of God.*
>
> —Matthew 15:6

The repetitive, mantralike chanting process has been a part

of many world wisdom traditions including Hinduism (*japam*),[19] Buddhism (*nembutsu*),[20] Yoga, Native American spiritualism, and even Catholicism. Rosaries or prayer beads are often used as an aid to this practice, sometimes with mystically beneficial results. Nichiren-Shoshu Buddhism's focus on the phrase "Nam-Myoho-Renge-Kyo" (Sanskrit for "The Sutra of the Perfect Law of the Lotus," but generally understood to mean "I devote my life to the Mystic Law of the Lotus Sutra")[21] still flourishes today world-wide, as does Tibetan Buddhism's practice of chanting "Ohm."

As to myself, even though I'd never been one to chant and had put away my rosaries long ago, I came to understand that there is a natural part of us that wants to play the song of the universe in our soul over and over again, for it is magnificent. I also came to understand that words or acts of adoration are of *giving*, not *getting*. Although I felt God deserved much more, I had nothing else to give but my worship.

It seemed little more than a week had passed since I'd begun to see my Father again. On this particular morning in late July, I was doing laundry when suddenly I began to feel a tremendous psychic or spiritual pain.

In trying to focus inner vision to find the source of this agony, I discerned it was coming from the world—one place, then another, then another. The more I looked, and the more I could see, the more I felt this incredible *pain* in my being—as if every part me were feeling the pain of others, people I didn't even know.

Why was I hearing these cries for mercy from my brothers

and sisters? Why was there violence and agony in the world? It made no sense. But even as I questioned, it all grew nearer. Hundreds were moaning, screaming, yet I had no hands to cover my eyes or ears. The more they screamed, the more I hurt.

As I carried clean laundry from one room to another, the walls of my house strangely posed no visual obstruction; I could see inside and out. The world was everywhere, and those suffering people were no longer my brothers and sisters, but my children. I had experienced visions before, but had always pulled back. This time, however, I could not—there was nowhere for me to go. The distance between me and the rest of the world had become nonexistent. I had to accept what I was now seeing: the unimaginable suffering of souls who did not know why they were in agony, where lack of understanding was as painful a part of their suffering as whatever else they endured. "Why? Why?" they cried.

I did not know the answer. And the more I searched, the closer everything came. As my mind saw the cruel transgressions that human beings can inflict upon one another—torture, war, killing, and on, and on—I reeled with the anguish felt by all of us. I felt as if the heart of every human being had become one heart, and that heart was within me.

As the barrier between myself and others burst asunder, I knew this was the same barrier that had been between myself and God. This sorrowful experience lasted only a few minutes, but during those moments I peered into hell and at the same time had a direct intercourse with God. The answers were placed before me.

The first thing I understood was our blindness and the hurt-

ful things we do because of it, the selfishness we exhibit, the pain
we all inflict upon one another, and how foolish it all is. I saw we
are all a part of this family that does not know it is a family.

The second thing was *felt*: the pain God endures because
we are oblivious of him. He literally sees all action from Reality,
and in so seeing, he knows he is not seen—that Reality is not
seen—and there is a part of him that wants us to know him. If
words could be put to this experience (I am pretending to be
God's ventriloquist!), they might be, "My children, you do not
know who you are, do you? I have placed myself before you,
beneath you, and above you. I have made you from within me
and surrounded you. Your feet walk upon my skin and I cradle
you in your dreams. I am here, and if only you could see me, you
would know."

The third thing I realized was the great love that binds each
person to the rest of humankind. This vision was conveyed from
God's overview of our existence. The indestructible bond of love
between God and humankind is as strong for one soul as it is for
all. Love is not quantitative; it is boundless. We are not only equally
endowed with that love, but we are equally endowed with the ability
to have *all* that love without taking one iota of it away from another. So great is God's love that his being is complete only with
each one of us. This is how much we are loved—and more.

The next thing I saw was forgiveness, the living act of grace
that allows humankind to change, to grow beyond the pain of
existing in blindness. This forgiveness is not given only to the
few who would ask for it; it is forgiveness that God gives the
moment a hurtful act is committed. Because every act is seen
from God's eye, that very *seeing* is forgiveness. God sees nothing

but perfection; thus, all things are made perfect by his seeing. He bears the pain of our ignorance; we only share in it. The greatest forgiveness of all is that which God gives to humankind for being oblivious of him and his love. The Lover does not stop loving because we are unaware of the source of his love. This is the living act of forgiveness, and it stems from the bond of love. This bond is a *commitment* God has made to all. Because this commitment is a part of his very being, it can never be broken. It is eternal, as is God's forgiveness.

As feelings of magnitude stretched my heart to embrace my mind—which had now become the world—I was safeguarded by this *commitment*. I could see the compassion God has for humankind. God experiences every hint of pain from every individual ever created from the beginning of time (as we may measure time) throughout all eternity. And he experiences that pain unto himself—*as* himself.

The chakra atop my head was moving around, almost jumping. I tried to ignore it because I wanted this experience to stop. Yet I knew there was no way out but through acceptance. I continued folding laundry as I stood near a chair in the spare bedroom. Stacked upon the chair were my clean towels, but I still had one in my hand that needed folding. I was crying.

As my hands gently folded the towel, tears streaming down my face, the words *inner universe* softly reverberated in my mind. I knew I'd heard those words before, but I could not remember where. I felt instinctively that they would lead me away from my present suffering.

I looked inside my mind and the "inner universe"—a huge, soft, almost malleable macrocosm—was there before me. Thrilled,

I felt like a child who had been freed to play in the biggest and best playground of all: the *cosmos*. For a moment I stopped at the entrance because it was not yet open. Then, instantly, my brain seemed to split and fold inward upon itself. A tremendous force pulled me even as I willed myself in.

I was then out of my physical body (although I didn't know it yet, for it all happened so fast), joined to a circle of people suspended in the dark like a ring of paper dolls against the night sky. There were many of us. We were holding hands. Everyone in the circle was connected. Suddenly a powerful bolt of lightning shot through all of us—I was electrified. At the very same time, my being was exploded to the outer reaches of the universe. I was *everything*—every particle, every space, every person, every animal, everything in existence. All was *me* and *I* was all that existed.

The next thing I knew was darkness, and I was alone. I had the feeling of being contained within a form that had nothing outside it but empty black space. I was out of my body again, only this time I'd gone too far out—I didn't know where I was. One moment I was the universe; the next, I was just me. Alone. Frightened.

Frantic, I immediately returned to my body through my top chakra, like a genie back into a bottle. Still standing there with the towel in my hand, I felt as if I'd been electrocuted. But instead of vibrational or pulsating jolts, this onrush was uninterrupted, galvanizing, and solid in its penetration—again, like lightning. The physical memory—tingling—was especially concentrated at the top of my head.

There was, however, a problem: the top of my head was

gone—as if someone had removed my cranium and just left a huge opening there. I could feel this opening for it tingled, and I could see through it as if it were an enormous third eye. What I saw was myself. I was in a place above, beyond my physical body, and I was below, on this earthly plane. There were two of me in two places at once, but those two places both felt like *here* to me. There was an exact mirror reflection—odd as it seemed—of here and there as both being *here*.

I began to try to make sense of what had just happened, I couldn't. The answers came before the questions. I was filled with all of creation. It was me, I was it. There was no difference.

Somehow I then knew what had happened. I had just experienced the great Oneness that is said to bring complete enlightenment. I'd read about it many times but never had I imagined that it would be like this! It should be given a new name, I thought—more like the "Electrifying Oneness." I'd had the greatest physical climax of all time with the greatest body of all time—the cosmos. It was the explosion of Self within the universal body of God. It was union with the Absolute, our Creator.

It was wonderful to have finally experienced it, yet it was agonizing wonder. Although I was eager to continue life being enlightened, I really didn't like the feeling of being the entire universe, nor did I like having two of me. Exceedingly frightened at what had happened, I turned again to God for help—I knew I could not handle this on my own. I implored, "Father, whatever happens, please do not let me be alone. I do not want to be all there is. I do not want to be you!" I just wanted me to be *me* and him to be *him* again, but the familiar silence I had come to know so well prevailed.

I was still in aftershock, with laundry in hand, when it occurred to me that I was late for work. *This is good*, I thought, glad
to have the common sense to know what I was supposed to do
here on Earth. I didn't know, however, if I was actually capable of
doing it, because there were still two of me. As I/we got ready to
leave, I/we wondered what the world outside would be like, considering what had happened.

I don't remember driving to work, but somehow I made it
there. As I got out of my car and started walking north on Broad-
way, the feeling I was *all* of creation gradually transitioned into
one of creation being the *rest* of me—as of I were becoming conscious of a Self that existed both beyond and within the universal
experience. I almost felt a budding of self-confidence as I glanced
across the busy street and into the eyes of an elderly man. He was
wearing a hat like those worn by men in the Irish countryside—
gray, with a small brim and flat top.

When our eyes met, I saw myself. *He* was *me!* There was
absolutely no difference between us, not even physically. I was
wearing that same gray hat and standing on the north side of the
street simultaneous to being myself on the south side of the street.
While hesitant to make eye contact with others—I knew they
were also me—I could not completely resist the temptation. I felt
like a person who has been blind her entire life and suddenly
gained full vision. But the problem with this vision was that all I
could see was *myself.*

I had never felt so lonely and so overwhelmed in my life. I
had to admit, however, that I had asked for enlightenment and
had gotten it. But once it had come, I wasn't sure I wanted it. I
did not want to be the only person in the world—for everyone

else to be me. I wanted company, and someone to turn to when I was in need. I felt like burning every book I'd ever read, erasing every memory, and starting all over, but I knew that was not possible. I was angry, disappointed, crazy with fear, and confused about what was going to happen next. I certainly did not want to experience that Electrifying Oneness again. I just wanted to be normal. I wanted my individuality back!

But there were still two of me: one pleading to remain an individual, and the other understanding the Absoluteness. I knew I could have dropped my body on the spot and gone into the Oneness, for that is what I was. Yet there was within me this strong desire to remain on Earth as an individual. I didn't care if it *was* illusion.

Many consider it blasphemy for one to say he is God; but in truth it would be blasphemous for me to say I am not God.

—**Meher Baba**[22]

The store was already open and bustling with customers as I approached the door. I was fighting to stay in my body and frightened the Electrifying Oneness would happen again. Yet with every thought came knowledge of the mechanical workings of the universe that seemed to pull me upward to the heavens. It seemed my own mind had been eradicated—all that was left was the universe around me, and that universe (including thought and feeling) was showing me how it worked. This understanding, however, imparted the feeling that I was being shaped into form—as if each aspect of creation had a beingness about it *from* which I was inseparate and *into* which I was molding myself.

Even so, I needed to function at work without appearing

detached. As a full breath of air entered my lungs, I made one last prayer for normalcy, opened the door, and walked to the back of the store, where Pete was sitting. Without knowing exactly why, I felt the urge to tell at least one person what had happened to me. I began to tell Pete about my experience.

As the words came out of my mouth, I was surprised at how calm they sounded, how matter of fact, how succinct—as if nothing important had happened. I spoke of doing laundry when suddenly, as lightning shot through all of us in the circle, I went out of my small body and became the entire universe and everyone in it. I also told him I felt there were now two of me, that I had a new sense of understanding about creation, and (so as not to upset him) that I would be OK. Pete nonchalantly responded, "That's nice."

For a moment I was taken aback with such a bland rejoinder. Pete knew about my lifelong hope to become enlightened, and I had thought perhaps he would be happy for me. But I guess he didn't understand that I had experienced the most absolute experience any human being can have: *I had become one with the Absolute*. And that Absolute was my true Self, the *only* Self—the Self of *all*. And yet, what should I have expected Pete to say? While there may have been a small part of me that wanted affirmation, in the end I knew congratulations would have served no purpose. So the conversation ended.

I began to set my mind on work when, all of a sudden, I had an irresistible urge to laugh. Everything seemed to strike me as hilariously funny and absolutely unimportant. I actually had to contain myself from taking all of the money out of the cash register, throwing it into the air, and telling everyone to look at it as just paper, green paper with no value whatsoever.

But I knew Pete and the patrons of the store would not understand. I knew I could not say to the next person walking through the door, "Hey, guess what I found out today? You are me and I am you. By the way, do you know that you are the universe? What do you think of *that*?"

I was, however, a little disappointed there would be no more search, for I knew the perennial quest that had ruled my life for as long as I could remember would be missed. Yet I was also relieved that my journey was over. I was ready to sit back and let enlightenment tell me what to do, where to go, and how to act. I was sure it would solve my problems, answer all my questions, and give me eternal joy, and that I would then share that joy with the world!

After a few moments of blissful naiveté, I realized there was still work ahead. I had become the universe and didn't quite know what to do about it. I also knew everyone else was the universe. They were God, too, even if they didn't know it. *But why*, I wondered, *didn't they? Why didn't I, until now?*

I had no idea that in asking these questions, I had immediately embarked upon another journey. Only in *this* journey, I would not feel lost or alone, or worry about my sanity. The unknown had been redefined as the part of my being that would prepare me for the challenges that lay ahead. Life *with* enlightenment was about to begin . . .

Epilogue

And the beat goes on . . .

I SOMETIMES IMAGINE WHAT IT MIGHT BE LIKE TO RETURN TO THAT little room in my dormer apartment and place myself on the same spot where I entered the Oneness. Silly as it may seem, I even wonder if I left an opening there for others to enter, join hands in the circle of humankind, and become electrified with all of creation. But nearly three decades have passed since then and I don't even know if the house is still standing.

If my imaginary scenario were real, however, everyone could simply pass through this opening and become completely enlightened, and the world would be perfect. There would be no hunger, war, or discord in the whole of creation; no species would become extinct, no rivers would become polluted; no one would become ill, age, or die; and there would be nothing to fear—not even the unknown—because everyone would know everything. But that's not life, neither is it enlightenment, so I'm glad this scenario is only imaginary.

So what *is* enlightenment? Simply put, it is what we have left when everything else is out of the way. It is ordinary, everyday life! Before my journey into the unknown began, I must have read that same (typically Zen) message a few thousand times, but I did not *get* it. I kept looking for something better, something more. I was filled with desire and, without knowing it, trampling over the very thing for which I searched.

So desire is a two-edged sword: The same desire that we all have to want more *from* life is the same desire that leads us to greater understanding *of* life. The crux of the matter is, if we want what we already have, we are not asking for anything, we are merely wanting to want. Amazing! How subtle is the mind, how obedient, how limited—it won't tell us that the very act of *wanting* gets in the way of *receiving*. We may *think* we want this or that, but what we really want is for the object of our desire to become a *reality* to us. And that's what enlightenment does: it makes ordinary life *real*.

In the process of getting to this point, we lose something of our old self, our old sense of reality, and we may even sit on the precipice of "madness," but this is a perfect kind of madness, for it takes us into Reality. And that Reality is that the totality of experience is here and now, and it doesn't need to be *found*—we're smack dab in the middle of it! This world upon which we walk is our very consciousness. (And that's the message of the Zen koan I was fretting over when my inner journey began: In order to exemplify his understanding, Monk Jōshu took off his sandal, put it over his head, and silently walked out of the room.)

Our consciousness is center of everything that ever has been or ever will be created. It is Self, loving and eternal. Most of all, it is *real*. Our universe is an extension of this Self, of *our* Self. How then can anyone even begin to want more? There is nothing more than everything! This is the Oneness, which when experienced consciously, is *electrifying*.

So what does one *do* after this experience? Nothing but go on living life with its ups and downs, joy and pain, mystery and knowing. What else can be done? And this is where *peace* enters. The seeking is over. This is not to say, however, that there is no excitement. Since 1973, my life has been filled to the brim. I now have two grown sons of whom I'm very proud and a wonderful husband who not only treats me with kindness and respect, but loves sharing his life with me. This has included a bit of travel: I've rung temple bells in Japan, pounded sacred drums in China, and sounded gongs in Indonesia. I have seen antiquity come together with modernism, not only in Parisian museums or the streets of London, Rome, or Barcelona, but in the flowing waters of Thailand's Chaopraya River. I have spent time with those who have slept with rats and with those who have played with royalty, with those who work to help children evade forced labor and with those who labor over what should be worn to the next ball. And I'm grateful for all of it.

I am also grateful to have had the opportunity to share my experiences with you. Just as I wanted to dispel some illusions about what may be perceived as mental illness or "madness," I wanted to dispel some illusions about enlightenment. In the process, I realized your reading would not be all fun and games, so I would like to thank you for sticking with me through the difficult parts of my journey as well as express my hope that your own journey will be easier for having done so. I, too, have learned from the experience of writing this book, for in recounting, I had to relive, and in reliving, I relearned. It's been a great ride!

Meanwhile, I've never met a "guru" or been to an ashram. To me, a guru is a good parent, a wonderful teacher, or a neighbor upon whom we can rely when we need a cup of sugar; a great doctor, lawyer, dentist, or accountant, not to mention the artists and musicians in this world who work to give us renewed perspective. And I don't know what I would do without my garbage man, whom I'm so happy to see every Thursday morning; my mail lady, who delivers packages rather than postal notices; my mechanic, who doesn't fool me about what's wrong with my car; or my local grocer, who will bring me a bag of potatoes when my car is *really* broken. The greatest ashram of all is life itself, and we're all connected in this marvelously mundane, simple yet complicated everyday life.

Since nothing should end without a new beginning . . . stay tuned. *Perfect Madness* continues to be a work in progress. Book 2 is already in the writing. In it, besides shedding more light upon the Electrifying Oneness (which we *all* experience during sleep) and the empowerment for "actualization" that it provides, I will explore the metaphysical foundations of our being, including the scales of karma, the seventh Sufi plane of awareness (*haqiqat*), and the source of individuality itself—which I had to learn about in order to remain here—as well as the role God plays in consciousness *after* enlightenment. (Now, that's a party!)

In closing: About two years into the writing of this book, I was relaxing in my dining room with a morning cup of coffee when I saw an elderly man plodding across the sidewalk outside my window. His steps were frail, his spine hunched, and his head poised downward, yet he placed one foot in front of the other with the determination of a warrior. I wondered what his life had been like, what he had learned, and if he knew that within him he carried the universe, and without him, he was walking upon it. I then recalled a phrase my father often used:

"There but for the grace of God go I." Only, as usual, the words turned around in my mind to say, "There *with* the grace of God go I."

Until we meet again,

Donna

NOTES

CHAPTER 1

[1] Paul Reps and Nyogen Senzaki, comp. and trans., *Zen Flesh, Zen Bones: A Collection of Zen and Pre-Zen Writings* (Garden City, NY: Doubleday), 89.

[2] Perle Besserman and Manfred Steger, *Crazy Clouds: Zen Radicals, Rebels & Reformers* (Boston: Shambala, 1991), 116.

[3] William Johnston, *The Mystical Way* (London: Harper Collins, 1933), 101.

[4] Zenkei Shibayama, *Zen Comments on the Mumonkan*, trans. Sumiko Kudo (New York: Harper & Row, 1974), 15.

[5] William Johnston, ed., *The Cloud of Unknowing: And the Book of Privy Counseling* (New York: Doubleday, 1973), 136.

[6] Robert Linssen, *Living Zen*, trans. Diana Abrahams-Curiel (New York: Grove Press, 1988), 194–95.

[7] Walter Scott, ed. and trans., *Hermetica: The Ancient Greek and Latin Writings Which Contain Religious Or Philosophic Teachings Ascribed to Hermes Trismegistus* (Boston: Shambala, 1993), 139, 319.

[8] John Blofeld, trans., *The Zen Teachings of Huang Po: On the Transmission of Mind* (New York: Random House, 1958), 41.

[9] Kenneth Wapnick, "Mysticism and Schizophrenia," *The Journal of Transpersonal Psychology* 1, no. 2 (1969).

[10] R. D. Laing, *The Politics of Experience* (New York: Random House, 1967), 121.

[11] Ibid., 129.

[12] Ibid., 133.

[13] Lee Sannella, M.D., *The Kundalini Experience: Psychosis or Transcendence?* (Lower Lake, CA: Integral Publishing, 1992), 113.

[14] Ibid.

[15] Rammurti S. Mishra, M.D., *Fundamentals of Yoga: A Handbook of Theory, Practice, and Application* (New York: Crown Publishers, 1987), 191.

[16] Ibid., 15.

[17] Pierre Teilhard de Chardin, *The Divine Milieu* (New York: Harper & Row, 1968), 59.

[18] Evelyn Underhill, *Mysticism: A Study in the Nature and Development of Man's Spiritual Consciousness* (New York: Penguin, 1974), 268.

[19] Ernest Holmes, *The Science of the Mind* (New York: Dodd, Mead & Company, 1938), 614.

[20] B. K. S. Iyengar, *Light on Yoga* (New York: Schocken Books, 1979), 119.

[21] Mishra, *Fundamentals of Yoga*, 128.

[22] Roshi Philip Kapleau, *The Three Pillars of Zen: Teaching, Practice, and Enlightenment* (New York: Doubleday, 1989), 43.

[23] Besserman and Steger, *Crazy Clouds*, 106.

[24] Peter Lamborn Wilson and Nasrollah Pourjavady, trans. and commentary, *The Drunken Universe: An Anthology of Persian Sufi Poetry* (Grand Rapids, MI: Phanes Press, 1987), 95.

CHAPTER 2

[1] Yogi Ramacharaka, *Fourteen Lessons in Yogi Philosophy and Oriental Occultism* (Chicago: The Yogi Publication Society, 1931).

[2] Daisetz Teitaro Suzuki, *Essays in Zen Buddhism: Third Series* (New York: Samuel Weiser Inc., 1976), 24.

[3] Pat Rodegast and Judith Stanton, comps., *Emmanuel's Book: A Manual for Living Comfortably in the Cosmos* (New York: Bantam Books, 1987), 65.

[4] John Stevens, *Three Zen Masters: Ikkyu, Hakuin, and Ryokan* (New York: Kodansha International, 1993), 101.

[5] Kahlil Gibran, *The Prophet* (New York: Alfred A. Knopf, 1996), 68.

[6] Walter Scott, ed. and trans., *Hermetica: The Ancient Greek and Latin Writings Which Contain Religious Or Philosophic Teachings Ascribed to Hermes Trismegistus* (Boston: Shambala, 1993), 253.

[7] Jane Roberts, *Seth Speaks: The Eternal Validity of the Soul* (San Rafael, CA: New World Library, 1994), 74.

[8] Alan Watts, *The Art of Contemplation: A Facsimile Manuscript with Doodles* (New York: Random House, 1972), 5.

[9] Robert Linssen, *Living Zen*, trans. Diana Abrahams-Curiel (New York: Grove Press, 1988), 120.

[10] Ibid., 113.

[11] J. Krishnamurti, *Commentaries on Living: Third Series, From the Notebooks of J. Krishnamurti*, ed. D. Rajagopal (Wheaton, IL: The Theosophical Publishing House, 1990), 285.

[12] J. Krishnamurti, *The Awakening of Intelligence* (New York: Avon Books, 1976), 340.

[13] Yogi Ramacharaka, *The Spirit of the Upanishads: Or Aphorisms of the Wise* (Chicago: The Yogi Publication Society), 60.

[14] Maurice Frydman, trans., *I Am That: Talks with Sri Nisargadatta Maharaj* (Durham, NC: Acorn Press, 1992), 360.

[15] *Maharishi Mahesh Yogi On The Bhagavad Gita: A New Translation and Commentary with Sanskrit Text, Chapters 1 to 6*, trans. Maharishi Mahesh Yogi (Baltimore: Penguin, 1969), 432.

[16] Diasetz Teitaro Suzuki, *Essays in Zen Buddhism: First Series* (New York: Grove Press, 1961), 198.

[17] Evelyn Underhill, *Mysticism: A Study in the Nature and Development of Man's Spiritual Consciousness* (New York: Penguin, 1974), 227.

[18] William Johnston, *The Mystical Way* (London: HarperCollins, 1933), 69.

[19] Eknath Easwaran, trans., *The Upanishads* (Tomales, CA: Niligri Press, 1996), 230.

[20] Kieran Kavanaugh and Otilio Rodriguez, trans., *The Autobiography of*

St. Teresa of Avila (New York: Book-of-the-Month Club, 1995), 351.

[21] Krishnamurti, *Commentaries on Living: Third Series,* 104.

[22] Heinrich Dumoulin, *Zen Buddhism: A History,* vol. 1, *India and China*, trans. James W. Heisig and Paul Knitter (New York: Macmillan Publishing, 1994), 67.

[23] Roshi Philip Kapleau, *The Three Pillars of Zen: Teaching, Practice, and Enlightenment* (New York: Doubleday, 1989), 85.

[24] Scott, *Hermetica*, 431.

[25] Meher Baba, *The Everything and The Nothing* (Myrtle Beach, SC: Sheriar Press, 1989), 60.

CHAPTER 3

[1] Jean Dunn, ed., *Consciousness and the Absolute: The Final Talks of Sri Nisargadatta Maharaj* (Durham, N C: Acorn Press, 1994), 20–21.

[2] Sigmund Freud, "The Ego and the Id," in *Great Books of the Western World*, vol. 5, ed. Robert Maynard Hutchins (Chicago: William Benton, Encyclopedia Britannica, 1952), 717.

[3] Dunn, ed., *Consciousness and the Absolute,* 22.

[4] C. G. Jung, "On the Nature of the Psyche," *in The Basic Writings of C. G. Jung*, ed. Violet Staub de Laszlo (New York: Random House, 1959), 93.

[5] Alan Watts, *The Way of Zen* (New York: Random House, 1989), 171.

[6] Jane Roberts, *Seth Speaks: The Eternal Validity of the Soul* (San Rafael, CA: New World Library, 1994), 191.

[7] C. G. Jung, "Archetypes of the Collective Unconscious," in *The Basic Writings of C. G. Jung*, ed. Violet Staub de Laszlo (New York: Random House, 1959), 315.

[8] Jean Gebser, *The Ever-Present Origin*, trans. Noel Barstad with Algis Mickunas (Athens, OH: Ohio University Press, 1991), 347.

[9] C. G. Jung, "The Relations Between the Ego and the Unconscious," in

The Basic Writings of C. G. Jung, ed. Violet Staub de Laszlo (New York: Random House, 1959), 128.

10 Ibid., 127.

11 Ahmed Ali, trans., *Islam: The Qur'an*, in *Sacred Writings*, vol. 3 (New York: Book-of-the-Month Club, 1992.

12 Meher Baba, *God Speaks: The Theme of Creation and Its Purpose* (New York: Dodd, Mead & Company, 1973), 47.

13 Ibid., 126.

14 Huston Smith, *The World's Religions: Our Great Wisdom Traditions* (New York: Harper Collins, 1991), 5.

15 Joseph Campbell, *The Power of Myth: Joseph Campbell with Bill Moyers* (New York: Doubleday, 1988), 209.

16 Dunn, *Consciousness and the Absolute*, 108.

17 Robert Linssen, *Living Zen*, trans. Diana Abrahams-Curiel (New York: Grove Press, 1988), 130.

18 J. Krishnamurti, *Commentaries on Living: First Series, From the Notebooks of J. Krishnamurti*, ed. D. Rajagopal (Wheaton, IL: The Theosophical Publishing House, 1967), 196–197.

19 James Clavell, ed., *The Art of War by Sun Tzu* (New York: Doubleday, 1983), 16.

20 Carl Gustav Jung, M.D., *Psychology and Religion* (New Haven, CT: Yale University Press, 1966), 41.

21 Lee Sannella, M.D., *The Kundalini Experience: Psychosis or Transcendence?* (Lower Lake, CA: Integral Publishing, 1992), 96.

22 Eknath Easwaran, trans., The Upanishads (Tomales, CA: Niligri Press, 1996), p.125.

23 Walter Scott, ed. and trans., *Hermetica: The Ancient Greek and Latin Writings Which Contain Religious Or Philosophic Teachings Ascribed to Hermes Trismegistus* (Boston: Shambala, 1993), 387.

24 Yogi Ramacharaka, *Raja Yoga: Or Mental Development* (Chicago: The Yogi Publication Society, 1934), 3.

[25] Massao Abe, ed., *A Zen Life: D. T. Suzuki Remembered* (New York: Weatherhill, 1986), 31.

[26] Ibid.

[27] I. K. Taimni, *Man, God and the Universe* (Wheaton, IL: The Theosophical Publishing House, 1974), 407.

[28] Jung, *Psychology and Religion*, 112.

[29] Yogi Ramacharaka, *Lessons in Gnani Yoga: The Yoga of Wisdom* (Chicago: The Yogi Publication Society, 1934), 130.

CHAPTER 4

[1] Massao Abe, ed., *A Zen Life: D. T. Suzuki Remembered* (New York: Weatherhill, 1986), 34.

[2] Thomas Aquinas, *The Summa Theologica of Saint Thomas Aquinas*, in *Great Books of the Western World*, vol. 20, ed. Robert Maynard Hutchins (Chicago: William Benton, Encyclopedia Britannica, 1952), 909.

[3] *Maharishi Mahesh Yogi On The Bhagavad Gita: A New Translation and Commentary with Sanskrit Text, Chapters 1 to 6*, trans. Maharishi Mahesh Yogi (Baltimore: Penguin, 1969), 271.

[4] Ibid., 354.

[5] D. C. Lau, trans., *Lao Tzu: Tao Te Ching*, stanza 186 (New York: Penguin, 1963), 140.

[6] Thomas Cleary, foreword to *Understanding Reality: A Taoist Alchemical Classic by Chang Po-tuan*, trans. Thomas Cleary (Honolulu: University of Hawaii Press, 1996), xiii.

[7] Understanding Reality: *A Taoist Alchemical Classic by Chang Po-tuan*, trans. Thomas Cleary (Honolulu: University of Hawaii Press, 1996), 163.

[8] C. G. Jung, *Psychology and Alchemy*, trans., R. F. C. Hull (Princeton, NJ: Princeton University Press, 1980), 301.

[9] Jung, *Psychology and Alchemy*, 301.

[10] D. C. Lau, trans., *Lao Tzu: Tao Te Ching*, stanza 81 (New York: Penguin, 1984), 96.

[11] Walter Scott, ed. and trans., *Hermetica: The Ancient Greek and Latin Writings Which Contain Religious Or Philosophic Teachings Ascribed to Hermes Trismegistus* (Boston: Shambala, 1993), 351.

[12] Thomas Aquinas, *The Summa Theologica of Saint Thomas Aquinas*, in *Great Books of the Western World*, vol. 19, ed. Robert Maynard Hutchins (Chicago: William Benton, Encyclopedia Britannica, 1952), 255.

[13] Joseph Campbell, *The Power of Myth: Joseph Campbell with Bill Moyers* (New York: Doubleday, 1988), 67.

[14] Abe, *A Zen Life*, 46.

[15] Thomas Cleary, trans., *Shobogenzo: Zen Essays by Dogen* (Honolulu: University of Hawaii Press, 1991), 104–105.

[16] Sonja Bargmann, trans. and rev., *Ideas and Opinions: Albert Einstein* (New York: Crown Publishers, 1982), 295–296.

[17] J. Krishnamurti, *The Ending of Time: J. Krishnamurti and David Bohm* (New York: Harper Collins, 1985), 221.

[18] Scott, *Hermetica*, 353.

[19] Abe, *A Zen Life*, 29.

[20] Rammurti S. Mishra, M.D., *Fundamentals of Yoga: A Handbook of Theory, Practice, and Application* (New York: Crown Publishers, 1987), 80.

[21] *Maharishi Mahesh Yogi On The Bhagavad Gita*, 311.

[22] Mishra, *Fundamentals of Yoga*, 79.

[23] Aquinas, *Summa Theologica*, in *Great Books of the Western World*, vol. 20, 1029.

[24] Evelyn Underhill, *Mysticism: A Study in the Nature and Development of Man's Spiritual Consciousness* (New York: Penguin, 1974), 258.

[25] Cited from *The Oxford Dictionary of Quotations* (Oxford and New York: The Oxford University Press, 1980), 95.

26 Diasetz Teitaro Suzuki, *Essays in Zen Buddhism: First Series* (New York: Grove Press, 1961), 26.

27 Pierre Teilhard de Chardin, *The Divine Milieu* (New York: Harper & Row, 1968), 108.

28 Underhill, *Mysticism*, 254.

29 Ibid., 256–258.

30 Teilhard de Chardin, *Divine Milieu*, 110–111.

31 Meher Baba, *God Speaks: The Theme of Creation and Its Purpose* (New York: Dodd, Mead & Company, 1973), 128.

32 Ibid., 133.

33 Scott, *Hermetica*, 119.

CHAPTER 5

1 Tarthang Tulku, *Knowledge of Time and Space* (Berkeley, CA: Dharma Publishing, 1990), 316.

2 *The Esoteric Writings of Helena Petrovna Blavatsky: A Synthesis of Science, Philosophy and Religion* (Wheaton, Illinois: The Theosophical Publishing House, 1980), 198.

3 Jane Roberts, *Seth Speaks: The Eternal Validity of the Soul* (San Rafael, CA: New World Library, 1994), 343.

4 Fritjof Capra, *The Tao of Physics: An Exploration of the Parallels Between Modern Physics and Eastern Mysticism* (Boston: Shambala, 1991), 115.

5 Pierre Teilhard de Chardin, *The Divine Milieu* (New York: Harper & Row, 1968), 149.

6 Capra, *Tao of Physics*, 160.

7 Ibid., 146.

8 Diasetz Teitaro Suzuki, *Essays in Zen Buddhism: First Series* (New York: Grove Press, 1961), 201.

[9] Venerable Khenpo Palden Sherab Rinpoche, Prajnaparamita: *The Six Perfections*, trans. Venerable Khenpo Tsewang Dongyal Rinpoche (Boca Raton, FL: Sky Dancer Press, 1991), 100.

[10] Sonja Bargmann, trans. and rev., *Ideas and Opinions: Albert Einstein* (New York: Crown Publishers, 1982), 20.

[11] Ibid., 21.

[12] Teilhard de Chardin, *The Divine Milieu*, 120.

[13] Meher Baba, *The Everything and The Nothing* (Myrtle Beach, SC: Sheriar Press, 1989), 85–86.

[14] Roshi Philip Kapleau, *The Three Pillars of Zen: Teaching, Practice, and Enlightenment* (New York: Doubleday, 1989), 79.

[15] *Understanding Reality: A Taoist Alchemical Classic by Chang Po-tuan*, trans. Thomas Cleary (Honolulu: University of Hawaii Press, 1987), 170.

[16] Yogi Ramacharaka, *Lessons in Gnani Yoga: The Yoga of Wisdom* (Chicago: The Yogi Publication Society, 1934), 135–136.

[17] Ibid., 124.

[18] C. G. Jung, *Psychology and Alchemy*, trans. R. F. C. Hull (Princeton, NJ: Princeton University Press, 1980), 312.

[19] K. M. Sen, *Hinduism* (New York: Penguin, 1961), 80.

[20] Thomas Aquinas, *The Summa Theologica of Saint Thomas Aquinas*, in *Great Books of the Western World*, vol. 20, ed. Robert Maynard Hutchins (Chicago: William Benton, Encyclopedia Britannica, 1952), 1029.

[21] Walter Scott, ed. and trans., *Hermetica: The Ancient Greek and Latin Writings Which Contain Religious Or Philosophic Teachings Ascribed to Hermes Trismegistus* (Boston: Shambala, 1993), 177.

[22] D. C. Lau, trans., *Lao Tzu: Tao Te Ching*, stanza 56 (New York: Penguin, 1984), 82.

[23] Teilhard de Chardin, *Divine Milieu*, 148–149.

[24] Ibid., 120.

[25] J. Krishnamurti, *The Ending of Time: J. Krishnamurti and David Bohm* (New York: Harper Collins, 1985), 204.

[26] Jung, *Psychology and Alchemy*, 340.

[27] J. Krishnamurti, *The Ending of Time: J. Krishnamurti and David Bohm* (New York: HarperCollins, 1985), 204.

[28] C. G. Jung, *Alchemical Studies*, trans. R. F. C. Hull (Princeton, NJ: Princeton University Press, 1983), 36.

[29] *Maharishi Mahesh Yogi On The Bhagavad Gita: A New Translation and Commentary with Sanskrit Text, Chapters 1 to 6*, trans. Maharishi Mahesh Yogi (Baltimore: Penguin, 1969), 100.

[30] *Esoteric Writings of Helena Petrovna Blavatsky*, 426.

[31] Lee Sannella, M.D., *The Kundalini Experience: Psychosis or Transcendence?* (Lower Lake, CA: Integral Publishing, 1992), 110–111.

[32] Richard Wilhelm, *The Secret of the Golden Flower: A Chinese Book of Life* (London: Arkana, 1984), 76.

[33] Ajit Mookerjee, *Kundalini: The Arousal of the Inner Energy* (Rochester, VT: Destiny Books, 1991), 44.

[34] Rosalyn L. Bruyere, *Wheels of Light: Chakras, Auras, and the Healing Energy of the Body* (New York: Simon & Schuster, 1994), 145.

[35] Cited from Yogi Ramacharaka, *Raja Yoga: Or Mental Development* (Chicago: The Yogi Publication Society, 1934), 219.

[36] Rammurti S. Mishra, M.D., *Fundamentals of Yoga: A Handbook of Theory, Practice, and Application* (New York: Crown Publishers, 1987), 194.

[37] Alan Watts, from a taped speech, no source available.

[38] Bargmann, *Ideas and Opinions*, 24.

[39] Timothy Ferris, ed., *The World Treasury of Physics, Astronomy, and Mathematics* (Boston: Little, Brown and Co., 1991), 71, 78.

[40] Ibid., 99.

[41] Nick Herbert, Ph.D., *Faster Than Light: Superluminal Loopholes in Physics* (New York: Penguin, 1989), 3.

[42] David Bohm, *Wholeness and the Implicate Order* (New York: Routledge, 1995), 80.

[43] Ferris, *World Treasury of Physics, Astronomy, and Mathematics*, 808.

[44] Ibid., 98.

[45] Leon Lederman with Dick Teresi, *The God Particle: If the Universe Is the Answer, What Is the Question?* (New York: Houghton Mifflin Co., 1993), 201.

CHAPTER 6

[1] Kieran Kavanaugh and Otilio Rodriguez, trans., *The Autobiography of St. Teresa of Avila* (New York: Book-of-the-Month Club, 1995), 361.

[2] Saint John of the Cross, Doctor of the Church, *Dark Night of the Soul*, ed. and trans. E. Allison Peers (New York: Doubleday, 1990), 104.

[3] Kavanaugh and Rodriguez, *Autobiography of St. Teresa of Avila*, 327.

[4] Evelyn Underhill, *Mysticism: A Study in the Nature of Development of Man's Spiritual Consciousness* (New York: Penguin, 1974), 399–400.

[3] Daisetz Teitaro Suzuki, *Essays in Zen Buddhism: Third Series* (New York: Samuel Weiser Inc., 1976), 40.

[6] Diasetz Teitaro Suzuki, *Essays in Zen Buddhism: First Series* (New York: Grove Press, 1961), 68.

[7] Massao Abe, ed., *A Zen Life: D. T. Suzuki Remembered* (New York: Weatherhill, 1986), 62.

[8] Suzuki, *Essays in Zen Buddhism: Third Series*, 36.

[9] Heinrich Dumoulin, *Zen Buddhism: A History*, vol. 2, *Japan*, trans. James W. Heisig and Paul Knitter (New York: Macmillan Publishing, 1990), 317.

[10] Perle Besserman and Manfred Steger, *Crazy Clouds: Zen Radicals, Rebels and Reformers* (Boston: Shambala, 1991), 101.

[11] Abe, *A Zen Life*, 62.

[12] Suzuki, *Essays in Zen Buddhism: Third Series*, 27.

[13] Meher Baba, *God Speaks: The Theme of Creation and Its Purpose* (New York: Dodd, Mead & Company, 1973), 136.

[14] Ibid.

[15] Keith Crim, *Perennial Dictionary of World Religions* (New York: HarperCollins, 1989), 540.

[16] Baba, *God Speaks*, 136.

[17] Ibid., 135.

[18] Ibid., 137.

[19] Huston Smith, *The World's Religions: Our Great Wisdom Traditions* (New York: HarperCollins, 1991), 35.

[20] Heinrich Dumoulin, *Zen Buddhism: A History,* vol. 1, *India and China*, trans. James W. Heisig and Paul Knitter (New York: Macmillan Publishing, 1994), 67.

[21] Richard Causton, *Nichiren Shoshu Buddhism: An Introduction* (London: Rider, 1991), 97.

[22] Meher Baba, *The Everything and The Nothing* (Myrtle Beach, SC: Sheriar Press, 1989), 48.

BIBLIOGRAPHY

Abe, Massao, ed. *A Zen Life: D. T. Suzuki Remembered.* New York: Weatherhill, 1986.

Ali, Ahmed, trans. *Sacred Writings.* Vol. 3, *Islam:* The Qur'an. New York: Book-of-the-Month Club, 1992.

Aquinas, Thomas. *The Summa Theologica of Saint Thomas Aquinas.* In *Great Books of the Western World.* Vol. 19, *Thomas Aquinas I,* edited by Robert Maynard Hutchins. Chicago: William Benton, Encyclopedia Britannica, 1952.

———. *The Summa Theologica of Saint Thomas Aquinas.* In *Great Books of the Western World.* Vol. 20, *Thomas Aquinas II,* edited by Robert Maynard Hutchins. Chicago: William Benton, Encyclopedia Britannica, 1952.

Arnold, Sir Edwin. *The Light of Asia.* Wheaton, IL: The Theosophical Publishing House, 1971.

Baba, Meher. *The Everything and The Nothing.* Myrtle Beach, SC: Sheriar Press, 1989.

———. *God Speaks: The Theme of Creation and Its Purpose.* New York: Dodd, Mead & Company, 1973.

Bargmann, Sonja, trans. and rev. *Ideas and Opinions: Albert Einstein.* New York: Crown Publishers, 1982.

Besserman, Perle, and Manfred Steger. *Crazy Clouds: Zen Radicals, Rebels and Reformers.* Boston: Shambala, 1991.

Blavatsky, Helena Petrovna. *The Esoteric Writings of Helena Petrovna Blavatsky: A Synthesis of Science, Philosophy and Religion.* Wheaton, IL: The Theosophical Publishing House, 1980.

Blofeld, John, trans. *The Zen Teachings of Huang Po: On the Transmission of Mind.* New York: Random House, 1958.

Bohm, David. *Wholeness and the Implicate Order.* New York: Routledge, 1995.

Bruyere, Rosalyn L. *Wheels of Light: Chakras, Auras, and the Healing Energy of the Body.* New York: Simon & Schuster, 1994.

Buber, Martin. *I and Thou.* New York: Charles Scribner's Sons, 1970.

Campbell, Joseph. *The Power of Myth: Joseph Campbell with Bill Moyers.* New York: Doubleday, 1988.

Capra, Fritjof. *The Tao of Physics: An Exploration of the Parallels Between Modern Physics and Eastern Mysticism.* Boston: Shambala, 1991.

Causton, Richard. *Nichiren Shoshu Buddhism: An Introduction.* London: Rider, 1991.

Clavell, James, ed. *The Art of War by Sun Tzu.* New York: Doubleday, 1983.

Cleary, Thomas, trans. *Shobogenzo: Zen Essays by Dogen.* Honolulu: University of Hawaii Press, 1991.

———. *Understanding Reality: A Taoist Alchemical Classic by Chang Po-tuan.* Honolulu: University of Hawaii Press, 1996.

Crim, Keith, ed. *Perennial Dictionary of World Religions.* New York: HarperCollins, 1989.

Dumoulin, Heinrich. *Zen Buddhism: A History.* Vol. 1, *India and China.* Translated by James W. Heisig and Paul Knitter. New York: Macmillan Publishing, 1994.

———. *Zen Buddhism: A History.* Vol. 2, *Japan.* Translated by James W. Heisig and Paul Knitter. New York: Macmillan Publishing, 1990.

Dunn, Jean. ed. *Consciousness and the Absolute: The Final Talks of Sri Nisargadatta Maharaj.* Durham, NC: Acorn Press, 1994.

Easwaran, Eknath, trans. *The Upanishads.* Tomales, CA: Niligri Press, 1996.

Edinger, Edward F. *Ego and Archetype: Individuation and the Religious Function of the Psyche.* Boston: Shambala, 1992.

Ferris, Timothy, ed. *The World Treasury of Physics, Astronomy, and Mathematics.* Boston: Little, Brown and Co., 1991.

Feuerstein, Georg. *Structures of Consciousness: The Genius of Jean Gebser—An Introduction and Critique.* Lower Lake, CA: Integral Publishing, 1987.

Feynman, Richard P. *QED: The Strange Theory of Light and Matter.* Princeton, NJ: Princeton University Press, 1985.

Freud, Sigmund. "The Ego and the Id." In *Great Books of the Western World.* Vol. 5, *The Major Works of Sigmund Freud,* edited by Robert Maynard Hutchins. Chicago: William Benton, Encyclopedia Britannica, 1952.

Frydman, Maurice, trans. *I Am That: Talks with Sri Nisargadatta Maharaj.* Durham, NC: Acorn Press, 1992.

Gebser, Jean. *The Ever-Present Origin.* Translated by Noel Barstad with Algis Mickunas. Athens, OH: Ohio University Press, 1991.

Gibran, Kahlil. *The Prophet.* New York: Alfred A. Knopf, 1996.

Herbert, Nick, Ph.D. *Faster Than Light: Superluminal Loopholes in Physics.* New York: Penguin, 1989.

Holmes, Ernest. *The Science of the Mind.* New York: Dodd, Mead & Company, 1938.

The Holy Bible, Revised Standard Version.

Humphreys, Christmas. *Studies in the Middle Way: Being Thoughts of Buddhism Applied.* Wheaton: The Theosophical Publishing House, 1984.

Iyengar, B. K. S. *Light on Yoga.* New York: Schocken Books, 1979.

James, William. *The Varieties of Religious Experience: A Study in Human Nature.* New York: Penguin, 1958.

Johnston, William, ed. *The Cloud of Unknowing and the Book of Privy Counseling.* New York: Doubleday, 1973.

Johnston, William. *The Mystical Way.* London: HarperCollins, 1933.

Jung, C. G. *Alchemical Studies.* Translated by R. F. C. Hull. Princeton, NJ: Princeton University Press, 1983.

―――. "Archetypes of the Collective Unconscious." In *The Basic Writings of C. G. Jung.* Edited by Violet Staub de Laszlo. New York: Random House, 1959.

―――. *Mysterium Coniunctionis: An Inquiry Into the Separation and Synthesis of Psychic Opposites in Alchemy.* Translated by R. F. C. Hull. Princeton, NJ: Princeton University Press, 1989.

————. "On the Nature of the Psyche." In *The Basic Writings of C. G. Jung.* Edited by Violet Staub de Laszlo. New York: Random House, 1959.

————. *Psychology and Alchemy.* Translated by R. F. C. Hull. Princeton, NJ: Princeton University Press, 1980.

————. *Psychology and the East.* Translated by R. F. C. Hull. Princeton, NJ: Princeton University Press, 1978.

————. *Psychology and Religion.* Translated by R. F. C. Hull. New Haven, CT: Yale University Press, 1966.

————. "The Relations Between the Ego and the Unconscious." In *The Basic Writings of C. G. Jung.* Edited by Violet Staub de Laszlo. New York: Random House, 1959.

Kapleau, Roshi Philip. *The Three Pillars of Zen: Teaching, Practice, and Enlightenment.* New York: Doubleday, 1989.

Kavanaugh, Kieran, and Otilio Rodriguez, trans. *The Autobiography of St. Teresa of Avila.* New York: Book-of-the-Month Club, 1995.

Khan, Hazrat Inayat. *Cosmic Language.* Tucson, AZ: Omen Press, 1972.

Krishnamurti, J. *The Awakening of Intelligence.* New York: Avon Books, 1976.

————. *Commentaries on Living: First Series, From the Notebooks of J. Krishnamurti.* Edited by D. Rajagopal. Wheaton, IL: The Theosophical Publishing House, 1967.

————. *Commentaries on Living: Third Series, From the Notebooks of J. Krishnamurti.* Edited by D. Rajagopal. Wheaton, IL: The Theosophical Publishing House, 1990.

————. *The Ending of Time: J. Krishnamurti and David Bohm.* New York: HarperCollins, 1985.

Laing, R. D. *The Politics of Experience.* New York: Random House, 1967.

————. *Self and Others.* London: Penguin, 1971.

Lau, D. C., trans. *Lao Tzu: Tao Te Ching.* New York: Penguin, 1984.

Lederman, Leon, with Dick Teresi. *The God Particle: If the Universe Is the Answer, What Is the Question?* New York: Houghton Mifflin Co., 1993.

Linssen, Robert. *Living Zen*. Translated by Diana Abrahams-Curiel. New York: Grove Press, 1988.

Maharishi Mahesh Yogi. *Maharishi Mahesh Yogi On The Bhagavad Gita: A New Translation and Commentary with Sanskrit Text, Chapters 1 to 6*. Translated by Maharishi Mahesh Yogi. Baltimore: Penguin, 1969.

Mishra, Rammurti S., M.D. *Fundamentals of Yoga: A Handbook of Theory, Practice, and Application*. New York: Crown Publishers, 1987.

Mookerjee, Ajit. *Kundalini: The Arousal of the Inner Energy*. Rochester, VT: Destiny Books, 1991.

The Oxford Dictionary of Quotations. Oxford and New York: The Oxford University Press, 1980.

Pagels, Elaine. *The Origin of Satan*. New York: Random House, 1995.

Ramacharaka, Yogi. *Fourteen Lessons in Yogi Philosophy and Oriental Occultism*. Chicago: The Yogi Publication Society, 1931.

———. *Lessons in Gnani Yoga: The Yoga of Wisdom*. Chicago: The Yogi Publication Society, 1934.

———. *Raja Yoga: Or Mental Development*. Chicago: The Yogi Publication Society, 1934.

———. *The Spirit of the Upanishads: Or Aphorisms of the Wise*. Chicago: The Yogi Publication Society.

Reps, Paul, and Nyogen Senzaki, comps. and trans. *Zen Flesh, Zen Bones: A Collection of Zen and Pre-Zen Writings*. Garden City, NY: Doubleday.

Roberts, Jane. *Seth Speaks: The Eternal Validity of the Soul*. San Rafael, CA: New World Library, 1994.

Rodegast, Pat, and Judith Stanton, comps. *Emmanuel's Book: A Manual for Living Comfortably in the Cosmos*. New York: Bantam Books, 1987.

Saint John of the Cross, Doctor of the Church. *Dark Night of the Soul*. Translated and edited by E. Allison Peers. New York: Doubleday, 1990.

Sannella, Lee, M.D. *The Kundalini Experience: Psychosis or Transcendence?* Lower Lake, CA: Integral Publishing, 1992.

Scott, Walter, ed. and trans. *Hermetica: The Ancient Greek and Latin*

Writings Which Contain Religious Or Philosophic Teachings Ascribed to Hermes Trismegistus. Boston: Shambala, 1993.

Sen, K. M. *Hinduism.* New York: Penguin, 1961.

Shibayama, Zenkei. *Zen Comments on the Mumonkan.* Translated by Sumiko Kudo. New York: Harper & Row, 1974.

Smith, Huston. *The World's Religions: Our Great Wisdom Traditions.* New York: HarperCollins, 1991.

Stace, W. T. *Mysticism and Philosophy.* Los Angeles: Jeremy P. Tarcher, Inc., 1960.

Stevens, John. *Three Zen Masters: Ikkyu, Hakuin, and Ryokan.* New York: Kodansha International, 1993.

Suzuki, Daisetz Teitaro. *Essays in Zen Buddhism: First Series.* New York: Grove Press, 1961.

———. *Essays in Zen Buddhism: Second Series.* New York: Samuel Weiser Inc., 1976.

———. *Essays in Zen Buddhism: Third Series.* New York: Samuel Weiser Inc., 1976.

Taimni, I. K. *Man, God and the Universe.* Wheaton, IL: The Theosophical Publishing House, 1974.

Teilhard de Chardin, Pierre. *The Divine Milieu.* New York: Harper & Row, 1968.

Tulku, Tarthang. *Knowledge of Time and Space.* Berkeley, CA: Dharma Publishing, 1990.

Underhill, Evelyn. *Mysticism: A Study in the Nature and Development of Man's Spiritual Consciousness.* New York: Penguin, 1974.

Venerable Khenpo Palden Sherab Rinpoche. Prajnaparamita: *The Six Perfections.* Translated by Venerable Khenpo Tsewang Dongyal Rinpoche. Boca Raton, FL: Sky Dancer Press, 1991.

Wapnick, Kenneth. "Mysticism and Schizophrenia." *The Journal of Transpersonal Psychology* 1, no. 2 (1969).

Watts, Alan. *The Art of Contemplation: A Facsimile Manuscript with Doodles.* New York: Random House, 1972.

————. *Beyond Theology: The Art of Godmanship*. New York: Random House, 1973.

————. *Nature, Man, and Woman*. New York: Random House, 1970.

————. *The Way of Zen*. New York: Random House, 1989.

————. *The Spirit of Zen: A Way of Life, Work, and Art in the Far East*. New York: Grove Press, 1960.

Wilhelm, Richard. *The Secret of the Golden Flower: A Chinese Book of Life*. London: Penguin, 1984.

Wilson, Peter Lamborn, and Nasrollah Pourjavady, trans. and commentary. *The Drunken Universe: An Anthology of Persian Sufi Poetry*. Grand Rapids, MI: Phanes Press, 1987.

The Soul in the Computer:
The Story of a Corporate Revolutionary
by Barbara Waugh with Margot Silk Forrest
Forewords by Alan Webber and Joel S. Birnbaum

Miracle in Maui:
Let Miracles Happen in Your Life
by Paul Pearsall, Ph.D.
Foreword by Kumu Kawaikapuokalani Hewett

The Paradoxical Commandments:
Finding Personal Meaning in a Crazy World
by Kent M. Keith
Foreword by Spencer Johnson, M.D.

High Country:
The Solo Seeker's Guide to a Real Life
by David M. Alderman
Foreword by Jean Houston

Perfect Madness:
From Awakening to Enlightenment
by Donna Lee Gorrell

INNER OCEAN PUBLISHING publishes in the genres of self-help, personal growth, lifestyle, conscious business, and inspirational nonfiction. Our goal is to publish books that touch the spirit and make a tangible difference in the lives of individuals and their communities.

We have selected for our first list five books that reflect our company's goals, depict the process of personal growth that we encourage in ourselves and others, and express conscious business practices that we embrace. To order additional copies or read about our other titles, we invite you to visit us at:

www.innerocean.com

Aloha.

The Soul in the Computer:
The Story of a Corporate Revolutionary
by Barbara Waugh with Margot Silk Forrest
Forewords by Alan Webber and Joel S. Birnbaum

Miracle in Maui:
Let Miracles Happen in Your Life
by Paul Pearsall, Ph.D.
Foreword by Kumu Kawaikapuokalani Hewett

The Paradoxical Commandments:
Finding Personal Meaning in a Crazy World
by Kent M. Keith
Foreword by Spencer Johnson, M.D.

High Country:
The Solo Seeker's Guide to a Real Life
by David M. Alderman
Foreword by Jean Houston

Perfect Madness:
From Awakening to Enlightenment
by Donna Lee Gorrell